Praise for *The Mountain in the Sea*

Locus First Novel Award Winner
Arthur C. Clarke Award Finalist
Nebula Award Finalist
Ray Bradbury Award Finalist

'Nayler's masterful debut combines fascinating science and well-wrought characters to deliver a deep dive into the nature of intelligent life . . . As entertaining as it is intellectually rigorous, this taut exploration of human – and inhuman – consciousness is a knockout' *Publishers Weekly*, starred review

'This compelling debut is impossible to put down, a delightful embroidery of the rush of scientific discovery and the pain of isolation, asking hard questions about what society is and what it means to truly understand another creature'
Booklist, starred review

'Less a science-fiction adventure than a meditation on consciousness and self-awareness, the limitations of human language, and the reasons for those limitations, the novel teaches as it engages' *Kirkus Reviews*

'I loved this novel's brain and heart'
David Mitchell, author of *Cloud Atlas*

'A first-rate speculative thriller, by turns fascinating, brutal, powerful, and redemptive'
Jeff VanderMeer, author of *Annihilation*

'Ray Nayler has taken on the challenge of a near future that's less certain than ever, and made it gleam . . . What a ride; what a feeling; what a future'
Robin Sloan, author of *Mr. Penumbra's 24-Hour Bookstore*

ALSO BY RAY NAYLER

The Tusks of Extinction

The Mountain in the Sea

WHERE THE AXE IS BURIED

WEIDENFELD & NICOLSON

WHERE THE AXE IS BURIED

A NOVEL

RAY NAYLER

First published in the United States in 2025 by MCD, Farrar, Straus and Giroux

First published in Great Britain in 2025 by Weidenfeld & Nicolson,
an imprint of The Orion Publishing Group Ltd
Carmelite House, 50 Victoria Embankment
London EC4Y 0DZ

An Hachette UK Company

The authorised representative in the EEA is Hachette Ireland,
8 Castlecourt Centre, Castleknock Road, Castleknock, Dublin 15, D15 XTP3,
Republic of Ireland (email: info@hbgi.ie)

1 3 5 7 9 10 8 6 4 2

Copyright © Ray Nayler 2025
Book design by Abby Kagan

The moral right of Ray Nayler to be identified as
the author of this work has been asserted in accordance
with the Copyright, Designs and Patents Act of 1988.

All rights reserved. No part of this publication may be reproduced, stored in a retrieval system, or transmitted in any form or by any means, electronic, mechanical, photocopying, recording, or otherwise, without the prior permission of both the copyright owner and the above publisher of this book.

All the characters in this book are fictitious, and any resemblance to actual persons, living or dead, is purely coincidental.

A CIP catalogue record for this book is available from the British Library.

ISBN (Hardback) 978 1 399 62788 7
ISBN (Export Trade Paperback) 978 1 399 62789 4
ISBN (eBook) 978 1 399 62791 7
ISBN (Audio) 978 1 399 62792 4

Printed in Great Britain by Clays Ltd, Elcograph S.p.A

www.weidenfeldandnicolson.co.uk
www.orionbooks.co.uk

For everyone who has lost a country

Exiles feed on empty dreams of hope.
I know it. I was one.
—AESCHYLUS, *Agamemnon*

BOOK ONE: OBSERVATION SHADOW

Halfway around the world in North America there grows a creosote bush that began its life from a seed almost twelve thousand years ago. The creosote is not a single, continuous organism, but rather a clonal colony. The original stem splits and fragments over centuries into genetically identical segments, a ring of living tissue replacing the original stem once it dies.

After millennia, that creosote is now a ring of living plant tissue fifty feet in diameter, tapped into both its own living roots and the pathways its ancient roots carved into the soil over millennia.

But when the seeds of the creosote grew, they sprouted in places where the root systems of ice-age trees once led to deep water. When you look down onto the circles of the creosote forest you are looking not only at creatures who took root before the Mayan pyramids were built—you are also looking at a map of the ice-age forest that was there before the creosote came. A "ghost forest"—an extinct pattern inside which the present has grown.

Our human systems are trapped in these same extinct patterns. The tsar is dead. Long live the tsar.

—ZOYA ALEKSEYEVNA VELIKANOVA, *The Forever Argument*

1

ZOYA
The Federation

The axe cleaved the log in two. The cut halves tumbled off the block and fell among the other hacked arcs of wood on the dark earth.

Until this fifth season of her exile, Zoya had cut her own wood. She was proud of her ability to sink the splitting maul through the pith.

But this season, every blow she struck was off-angle. She struggled for an hour.

Finally her assistant interrupted:

"Zoya Alekseyevna, I do not like your vitals. Please stop. Let me do it for you."

Her muscles felt the same. Everything *felt* the same.

Maybe her will had failed her.

That was what she feared most. Chopping wood wasn't about strength or accuracy. You *willed* the axe through the pith of the wood. The physical action was a muscular extension of that, nothing more.

Now Zoya sat in her canvas chair and watched her robot assistant chop wood. There was nothing mechanical about its actions. The way it adjusted its stance and grip between blows, the way it balanced each new round on the block. The word that came to mind was "intelligence." The intelligence of the body. The effortless, accurate intelligence of a child jumping rope. It did not have will, did it? And yet, although each round of wood was different, the blow it struck was perfect every time. What the robot had, its perfect calculation, seemed better than human will. Or, at least, more efficient.

The woodcutting area was near the edge of the clearing. The sun came through the silver birch trees. It scattered coins of light onto the robot's burnished arms, onto the cut wood, raw as morning flesh.

Maybe to grow old well you had to allow others to take over your work. You had to know when your work had come to an end.

Zoya was trying.

She watched the scattered light on the robot's surface. She listened to the syncopation of the maul whunking through the rounds of wood, the clop of cleaved wood falling among the other wedges and half rounds.

The breeze was as warm as the air it moved. No winter to fear, yet.

She listened to the shudder of the arrowhead-shaped leaves of the birches, twisting on their petioles.

Then she saw the ghost.

It walked among the pale lines of the birch trees, deep in shadow.

A human figure against the stark tree trunks. But as it came, she could see the white bark of the birches cutting down through its body.

The ghost came steadily, a shadow among the chalk-line trunks, passing without obscuring them.

Here it comes. Not death, which I would have welcomed—but my mind's unraveling.

Then she covered her left eye. The ghost became solid as any person. It was twenty meters from the clearing.

She covered her right eye. The ghost was gone completely, removed from the world with not even a shimmer left behind to say it had been there.

But still there. She could hear its tread through the decomposing leaves. She could sense the silence of birds around it, tracking its movement through the taiga.

Zoya covered her left eye again. A woman emerged into the clearing. Her drab military backpack matched the tones of the rest of her outfit.

The woman placed a finger across her lips.

Both eyes open now, Zoya saw the woman as a translucent figure against the forest's edge. The sun came down through her. The leaves turned in the breeze beyond her glassy flesh.

Zoya stood up from her chair. "When you finish with the wood," she said to the robot, "stack it. Then gather mushrooms and check the hives."

"It will be done," the robot replied.

Zoya and the woman the robot could not sense crossed the clearing to the little log cabin at its center.

Inside, the cabin was cool and pleasant. It smelled of cedar. Light fell in trapezoids across clean floorboards. A whitewashed *pechka* dominated the room: stove and hearth, source of warmth and bread. The sound of the axe was inaudible once the door was closed.

"Tea?" Zoya asked.

"Yes, thank you." The woman looked around at the embroidered curtains, the polished surfaces, the gleaming samovar in its niche in the pechka's side.

"You are wondering if I embroidered all this. I did not. It is the robot's work. Sit." Zoya indicated a small table, its white tablecloth edged in a red and black pattern.

Zoya watched the woman's gaze settle on a small bookshelf.

"The classics, mostly," said Zoya. "Tolstoy, Turgenev, Pushkin—whom I still cannot stand. If you are looking for my book, it isn't there. It is forbidden even to me."

Zoya served the tea. They both sat down.

"I'm not frightened," Zoya said after a few moments.

The woman brought the cup of tea a few centimeters from her lips, blew across its surface. "What do you mean?"

"In Byzantium, they would blind the fallen emperors, strand them on an island, exile them to a monastery. They would do everything they could to stop short of regicide. But it was never enough. Their very *existence* nagged. The strangling cord is the only way the tyrant can live in peace, then or now. This state grew within Byzantium's mold. The President cannot let me live. It is not in his nature."

"I'm—"

"Don't protest. Drink your tea. I am not frightened. Quite

the opposite. I am ready. The President has murdered everyone I loved. Everyone who fought alongside me. I am the only one left. Do you know what that is like? To be the only one left? To wait for the bullet, the drone, the poison—and have it never come? It is worse than death."

Zoya let honey run into her cup from a spoon. "I thought you were a ghost. That I was losing my mind. That is what I have been afraid of most of all. That the President exiled me here so the isolation would tear my mind apart. But then I understood—you are real, but my digital eye cannot see you. Only my human eye can. The President did blind me: with a rubber bullet, in that protest decades ago, when I was still young. Just like in Byzantium. But he only half finished the job."

Zoya did feel calm. Her work was unfinished, yes. But in the end all work was unfinished. She paused, expecting the woman to speak, but the woman placed her cup of tea down on the table and waited.

"What is the mechanism?" Zoya asked. "How do you make yourself invisible to them?"

The woman drew a cylinder from her pocket. A green light glowed at its tip. "It is called a Birnam device. It maps the disturbance you create in the world and emulates the data that would exist in your absence. It doesn't make you invisible—it *replaces you* with what would be there if you were not. Like our own minds replace the blind spot in our vision with what should be there. But only machines are vulnerable to it. An acetylene torch against the electronic cage they put us in."

"Extraordinary."

The woman put the device back in her pocket. "I have read your book so many times, Zoya Alekseyevna: *'There is no solution to disagreement,'*" she recited. "*'There is no technology that can overcome it, no leader that can repress it. There is only the eternal flow of argument . . .'*"

"I have forgotten more of my book than I remember," Zoya said.

"That is one of my favorite passages," the woman said. "I have memorized so many of them. We all have."

"You aren't here to kill me."

"You seem disappointed."

No winter to fear, yet.

Except the one in the mind.

Winter, when the snow lay heavy in the clearing. When nothing but narrow paths ran through it—miniature mountain passes, cut between drifted peaks. When the world shrank until it was only her, in the dimness of the cabin, alone with her thoughts, and the robot, sitting in its wooden chair, working on a piece of embroidery.

"Tell me a story," she would say. And the robot would—but the stories it told were flat and characterless, even if on their surface they might seem the same as human stories. Its stories did nothing but make her feel more alone.

Was it as simple as that? Did she wish for death because she could not face another winter alone?

She had felt relieved, knowing her last moments had come.

Now that relief was gone. What did she feel? Afraid? No. Exhausted.

"It was an irony," Zoya said, "when the President imprisoned me here, in the taiga. Here, where I spent my early days on scientific expeditions. Where I believed I was forging an identity as a naturalist, not an activist. But exiling me here, and then not allowing me to wander the forest, was a particular cruelty. The taiga is scope and drama: summer rains that drown areas the size of France, late-spring snow that falls on places no human has ever seen. The grand struggle for existence. I cannot see it. And even if I were free to roam, it would be no good to me now. It has been stained."

"By what?"

"By a lifetime of human politics," Zoya said. "All I see are allegories everywhere for human behavior. I want to stop comparing the plants and animals to us, but I can't. And those comparisons are not fair to them. But if you are not here to kill me, then what is this? A visit? You came to see what is left of me, after all these years alone?"

"No, Zoya Alekseyevna. No." The woman covered Zoya's hand. Like a granddaughter would.

My book has been with her for so long. My words are etched in her. She feels she knows me.

It was the first human touch Zoya had felt in five years. She clasped the woman's hand in return.

"We need you again, Zoya Alekseyevna."

Something woke in Zoya at those words. Yes—there it was. She had survived these years in exile because of this. Because she had known—hadn't she?—that she would be needed again. That she would have a purpose again. She would be of use again.

"We need you," the woman said again, "but we cannot free you. So I have come to duplicate you."

2

LILIA
The Federation

"Citizen, can you come with me?"

The man wore the gray uniform of a people's safety warden.

Lilia followed him to the convenience annex. It was a booth so small that no more than one person could sit in it. A bamboo-paper cup of tea rested in a plastic holder on a narrow counter. Faces scrolled on the screens surrounding the swivel chair at the booth's center—faces in green-framed boxes, face after face of the people passing on the sidewalks for blocks around. In the corner of each screen rotated a golden icon of the President's face.

Hovering in the center of one of the displays was her own face, frozen in blank non-thought as she exited the convenience store. It had a yellow frame around it. A halo of other images also surrounded it—video stills of her waiting for a crossing light, of her walking down the sidewalk.

"Your name is Lilia Vitalyevna Rybakova."

"Yes."

"This is your personal identification number."

"Yes."

The warden held out a hand. "Your terminal."

He placed her terminal on the scanpad. It pulsed green: no forbidden apps, no contraband code.

The people's safety warden touched Lilia's image on the screen, tracing a shortcut glyph. An aerial view of the neighborhood came up, a grid of streets overlaid by circles. One circle was bright against the rest. A yellow dot outside its edge indicated her position. "You are in violation of your conditional release," the warden said. "You have strayed from your circumference."

"That can't be right. This is my regular store . . . I came here yesterday."

"Yes," he said. "I register that. Your circumference was reduced since then."

"For what? I haven't done anything."

The warden swiped another glyph on the screen, bringing up the multifactor rainbow of her social credit score. Next to it, a red arrow pointed down: –30 on the *positive influence on others* bar.

"I don't even understand what that could be."

The warden shrugged. "Perhaps you not understanding is the problem."

At home, Lilia put groceries away in the refrigerator. When she took the flour from the polymesh shopping bag and placed it on the counter, a small black dot crawled away from it. Then another.

She lifted the paper sack. It was riddled with insect holes. Infested.

Great, she thought. She had long ago learned not to say sarcastic things aloud. *And of course, now I can't even return it.*

"Papa?"

Vitaly was in the living room. The mandatory feedscreen muttered away, reduced to its lowest legal volume. Onscreen the President shook hands in a white and gold room. On the wall behind him was his portrait. His icon rotated in the corner of the screen.

Lilia called that a "three-in-one." Never aloud, of course.

Vitaly was asleep. The bottle of painkillers sat next to him on the tray table.

Thirty points gone from her social credit score. How had it happened?

"*I can't go to church today. The standing is killing me. The pain in my hip is too much.*"

"*Stay home, then.*"

Yes—that must be it. "*Stay home, then.*" Ten points a word.

Standing for more than an hour sent pain through the side of his body. It was difficult for him to bear without extra painkillers. But the painkillers affected his judgment. The last time he took them before church, he had almost laughed during the service, when a child stumbled out of place and got smacked in the butt with the thurible.

His stifled laughter had (hopefully) gone unnoticed—but such things couldn't be risked. So, the week afterward Vitaly had skipped the painkillers. He'd stood there in the cave of the church, pale as the martyrs frescoed into the plaster of the walls, a nauseated medieval green, gritting his teeth and crossing himself, beads of sweat rolling down his pain-creased face.

Stay home, then.

She could have said nothing.

No—fifteen points for silence, probably. Or maybe even the same thirty points. Who knows? Maybe more.

She should have argued with her father, tried to convince him he should go to church, but communicated somehow that she didn't mean it.

But maybe even that wouldn't have been enough.

Perhaps you not understanding is the problem.

There weren't any stores within her reduced radius. If they needed flour, Vitaly would now have to limp out to get it. If *his* social credit score was still high enough. They could not rely on the charity of neighbors: few would risk their own social credit to help a neighbor, not knowing how the authorities would view their assistance.

She wasn't sure he'd make it. His hip joint was failing. He was far down the line for a replacement.

The church was right around the corner, though. Maybe they could live on nothing more than incense and the platitudes half sung in Father Christophoros's baritone. Maybe they could live on the communion wafers they had to choke down every Sunday.

Maybe they could miracle some bread out of Father Christophoros's sonorous, baritone bullshit.

Speaking of bread—she went back into the kitchen. The ruined flour would have to be thrown away. Or could they even afford to throw it away? Would they have to eat it, bugs and all? Had it come to that?

The bag had a large hole in its corner, and flour had spilled out.

The flour was moving on the counter, swarmed by black dots.

Nausea surged through her.

Then words formed, the black dots pushing the flour into shape.

CONTROL EXPRESSION

She was already doing so. It was one of the things her country taught a person to do first.

The lines of text appeared, nudged into shape by the swarm of tiny bots, then smeared away. Each phrase was replaced by a new line, one after another.

BIRNAM DEVICE IN FLOUR SACK
WHEN READY
DEPRESS TIP TO USE
TAN LADA NIVA ACROSS FROM PLAYGROUND
MUST BE TODAY
TAKE NOTHING
REMEMBER NOT ALL SURVEILLANCE ELECTRONIC
IF CAUGHT
BIRNAM DEVICE IS DEATH SENTENCE

After smearing the last line away, the black dots streamed into the sink and down the drain.

They could read her pulse with the cameras, of course. Read it via the change of blood flow to her skin, invisible to the naked eye. But an elevated pulse could be caused by almost anything—they knew she had been told, minutes before, that her circumference had been reduced. She might be thinking about that. That would account for the nausea she had experienced as well. The cameras would see nausea.

She opened the refrigerator, pretending to take inventory.

Where were the cameras? Yes—the bag of flour, and the text that had been written, was in a blind spot.

A Birnam device. The programmers she'd worked with in London, where she had been studying until six months ago (had it been that short a time? Six months, and a lifetime), had called them "portable holes." None of them had ever seen one. They cost, it was rumored, a few million pounds each.

Who would take that kind of risk on her?

And of course, having one here was a death sentence.

A death sentence, or a way out.

A choice.

But given to her by whom?

She crossed the tiny kitchen and looked out the window, giving herself time to think.

The city stretched off into the distance, composed of unlike fragments: an onion dome, the gray skeleton of an office tower rising over rotting red-tile roofs, a scabrous line of apartment blocks. There was a hideous ten-story building they used to call the "dinosaur." Clad in prefabricated green tile panels, it lay like the peeling corpse of a brontosaurus near the central park.

The city looked almost the same as it had twenty years

ago. Except for the intrusion of a blue-glass tower and a newer block of apartments reserved for apparatchiks, clad in dull white plastimarble, the view was no different from the view of her childhood.

From here, you couldn't see the convenience annexes gridded through the streets. You couldn't see the invisible loops limiting the movements of those on "conditional release." Those circles were the city's true geography. Overlapping orbits of limitation.

In London, they had said half the Federation's citizens were on conditional release. Of course, those numbers were the guesswork of international NGOs and "foreign agents" pushed into permanent exile decades ago.

Guesswork, but probably accurate enough.

Sometimes, walking down the street, she imagined she could tell who the people on conditional release were. They were the ones minding their steps a little more. They were the ones checking their terminals a bit too often, watching the map of their perimeter to make sure they didn't stray over the edge.

You were always about to stray. You always walked right up to the edge of your circle. At the zoo, as a child, Lilia remembered watching the polar bears pace back and forth in front of the glass. They gouged barren streaks in the grass of their enclosures. The boundary line. And the other animals—the tigers, the monkeys, the lions—they did it too.

They were marking the edge of where they *could* be. The edge of their terrain. *I can go this far. Here, but no farther.*

The instinct of any animal. *And what I want is to go farther.*

That was the hidden city. The real city: the city of circles. Some were larger than others, encompassing most of the city. Others were the size of a neighborhood. Some were no larger than a city block. Smaller and smaller, like flecks of foam on a wave. Overlapping with one another, or inside one another. Within each noose the little dot traced its arc along the border.

If the buildings disappeared, if the city were a grassy field, the people walking their circles would rut their edges right into the soil itself. Their imprisonment would be visible to satellites as an arced calligraphy paced into the ground.

She found herself thinking, again, of London. The London in her mind was a university quad dusted with snow. The sound of church bells from an unseen cathedral. She was there, with her terminal tucked under her arm and her breath a cold crystal cloud, hurrying. Going somewhere. Other students hurried here and there under a sunset sky, cutting paths through snow stained the color of the sunset clouds.

London was not like that all the time—not nearly. Almost never. But it had been like that for a moment. And it always *felt* like that to her, in her memories of it, now that it was a place she could never return to.

Or could she? Was it possible that the Birnam device, the message carved out of flour by that swarm of insect nanobots, was the opening of a door—the beginning of a return?

Her home was not here. Her home was in London. She had felt that as soon as she stepped off the plane here. Her father was here, but her home no longer was. She had come to say goodbye forever.

And then—this. Her freedom had been so fragile. Cut

from paper. All it took to make it disappear was a visit to her father.

She had left Palmer at the airport, thinking she would hardly have time to miss him. She would be back in two weeks.

She'd waved goodbye to him while the security tube angled its blades of light over her. Nothing but a twitch of her finger while the machine blatted at her to stay still.

One last visit to her father, and she could commit to freedom completely.

She had barely stepped off the plane when she felt the hand on her shoulder.

She sat in a plastic chair in a police station, still fantasizing about her "rights." Rights she'd left back there, along with her new life.

They broke her terminal's encryption in five hours. She had thought it was perfect. They had found a vulnerability in her system that was more perfect. A zero-day vulnerability that had probably been built into every terminal in the world, waiting for this moment to trap her.

The only illicit thing on her terminal was a secure chat app she used to communicate with Palmer. Her only link to him. She had risked it, because she felt—what? That there had to be something, a thread at least, left to connect them. That she might, otherwise, become lost forever. She had promised herself she would message him no more than once a day. Every few days, even. As little as possible, to avoid detection.

A minuscule risk, she told herself. A way of assuring herself that she would come back from behind the Federation's firewall. Home was London, and Palmer, and she needed that link.

A lifeline.

A forbidden Western app.

At the moment of her arrest, she remembered a passage from *The Forever Argument*:

From that moment, we understood that the state was everywhere. The state did not need to anticipate us: it was always with us. It shaped the mistakes we would make, and it was there to take us into its prisons when we made them.

When they put her in the back of the van, she thought it would be the Public-Private Enterprise Camps, the PPECs, for sure. Or worse.

But the van sat in a parking lot until a people's safety warden opened the back door, handed her scrubbed terminal to her, and told her she would be placed on "conditional release." Details uploaded to her terminal, including the exact limits to her freedom of movement, expression, and entertainment. He read off the applicable codex. Thank you, and have a good day.

The van dropped her at her home address and sped away to process the next citizen.

She had known, walking up the steps, entering the half-light of the stairwell she had run up and down so many thousand times as a child, that she would never see her life in London again. Never see Palmer again.

And when her father opened the door, and she saw the look of horror on his face at seeing her back here, she knew how enormous the mistake she had made was.

She had destroyed everything, and there was no way back. No possible way to make amends.

Standing in her kitchen, Lilia picked up the mesh shopping bag. She reached into the burst bag of flour. The Birnam device was there.

But where could she disappear? She knew: Near the garbage cans behind the building, there was a blind spot. The children who played in the courtyard had found it. It was where they gathered for their more secret games.

The children always knew where there were no cameras.

She slung the mesh bag over her shoulder.

She did not say goodbye to her father. She could not. On any other day she would not wake him to say goodbye, if she were only going out for groceries. This had to look like any other day.

Near the rear of the building, Lilia Vitalyevna Rybakova walked out of the range of camera 0275-0q37858, passing into what technicians termed an "observation shadow." Three seconds later, judging by her pace, she should have come back into view, picked up by camera 0275-0q37878.

She never did.

3

PALMER
The Union

They left Palmer sitting in a metal folding chair in a hallway for two hours. The light through the grime-frosted windows was grayer than the sky outside.

Palmer had never been to this exact part of London, but he had seen so many places like it. He worked in a London like this—decommed manually driven trucks lined up behind concertina wire, vacant lots of waste ground, buildings of cracked stucco, peeling tile, rain-stained concrete, mossy brick.

Eventually, some corporation would buy all this up. It would scrape the ground clean and drop in a prefabricated fulfillment center a hundred times the size of anything that had been here before, lit up cold LED white at night. There would be an autoshuttle to bring workers like Palmer in.

But past the fence line, there were always places like this, left over from an earlier time. This was how Palmer and every other warehouse worker started and ended every workday: staring at the dead windows of the past.

Palmer sat in the chair and watched dull sunlight crawl up the wall. He had sweat through his shirt. On the surface, he felt calm—but he knew it was false, a skein over his anxiety. The sweat told the truth. Everything relied on what happened next. On them believing him.

Finally, the door opened. The woman put out a hand. Later he would remember that—her warm hand where there had only been the chill of dead industry.

The furniture looked salvaged: a heavy green metal desk, some old-fashioned lamp with a thick cord running to a socket in the wrong place on the wall. There was another folding chair for him to sit in. Nothing on the walls but the rectangular shadows of grime where frames had once hung.

When she sat down, her high-backed leather chair loomed over her. She folded her hands on the desk and said, "Tell me your story."

Palmer hesitated.

The woman said, "You are trying to decide what you do and don't want to share with me. But if you want Lilia back, you need to tell me every detail. You won't know *which* details are important."

"*Can* you get her back?"

"Start with telling me your story. We'll go from there."

Later, on the upper deck of the bus, up front with his feet against the rail, Palmer felt the comedown from talking. The bus angled through the city's night gloom, the streetlights smeared by rain. The sickness in Palmer's stomach was made worse every time the bus guided itself around a corner in its rough, inhuman way.

It had felt good to talk about it all. For months, nobody had listened to him. He'd dragged his story from one government office to another. He'd shown them Lilia's last messages, told them how she had gone back to see her father one last time. How they lost contact just after she landed. How she had a return ticket already purchased, already paid for, but never got on the plane. She was coming back.

"Maybe she just didn't want to return," one of the government bureaucrats said.

But she hadn't walked away. She had been *taken*. That was what he had been trying to tell them for months, in one office after another.

No one listened.

Until he got a call from the woman. A promise to hear him out.

"I don't understand why nobody cares," he told her on the phone. "A person is gone. A person disappeared. And maybe she isn't a citizen here—but that doesn't mean she's no one. That doesn't mean she isn't *human*."

"*We* care. That's why I'm calling."

In the end, in that bleak office, he'd told the woman everything.

He'd started from when he and Lilia met in a nameless ruin bar at an Eastern European steel plant, where you could sit in a poncho and drink craft beers as the rain poured down through the bomb and shrapnel holes of a gone war and the music thumped.

Tourists had covered everything in the ruin bar in graffiti. Their names, dirty pictures, attempts to be deep about life, commentary about the terrible things that had happened here—things they tried to care about but didn't. A Buddha with an AK-47 slung over his shoulder was painted on the wall. Someone's attempt at depth or irony. A hundred tourists had scrawled their names on his body.

Lilia standing at the foot of a stairwell with a pint in one hand and that book *The Forever Argument* in the other. Looking right, looking left. Seeing him. Seeing him see her, joining him at his table as if she had *recognized* him.

He remembered the table they sat at: a giant wooden industrial spool, pockmarked by bullet holes. Someone had sanded all the splinters down, to make sure you didn't jab yourself while you drank.

That was what history was like everywhere he traveled: someone had sanded the splinters down.

He was watching other people have a good time, under the strings of colored lights. Remembering the scene later, it felt as if he were waiting for her. But he hadn't been waiting for her—he'd been waiting for anything at all.

She sat down at the table. He asked her about the book.

"I'm afraid to open it," she said. "It is forbidden in my country—but as soon as I stepped off the plane, I saw a copy in English in the airport bookstore and bought it. That was yesterday. I am still afraid. I just carry it around . . . In my country—in the Federation—it is a death sentence to read it. It's a death sentence to say a sentence from it out loud."

"So, it's not *The Little Prince*."

"I do not know what *The Little Prince* is."

A few minutes later, she said, "I'd like to leave here."

"Why?"

She gestured at the bullet holes, the bear-claw marks of artillery rounds. "My country did this to these people. I hate that people are wandering around in this place, happy here. People who never cared about any of this."

From that moment they were together. Together they moved from one hostel to another, along the new backpacker trails, where you could safely drink your beers and your shots while admiring the scars of old wars and poverties.

They walked together along the seawalls where you could dream of the natural beaches there before the ocean took them back.

Behind the seawalls were the ersatz white sand beaches dumped from the backs of autotrucks. Sunburned people picked their way down the hot metal stairs and plunged into the surge of the sea.

"Why did you choose me?" he asked her once, months later.

"You were the most English person I'd ever seen."

In London, they saw each other every day. She was on a scholarship slightly less miserly than his wages. They found a flat. They bought a few pieces of furniture.

They entered into a relationship by doing things, without ever talking about what they were doing or why.

It was difficult to explain it to the woman in the dreary room. Things had just . . . happened, without Palmer or Lilia making them happen.

In fact—and the woman had pointed this out to him in the middle of their conversation—there was a lot he and Lilia never discussed.

It made sense to him at the time—she did not talk to him about her country, because talking about it was painful. She did not talk to him about her studies or her work because he would not understand it. It was all math and computers.

He didn't know computers. To him, they were the things that told him which location to proceed to next in the warehouse. They told him when he wasn't walking fast enough, and when he could take his break. They told him when he was allowed to go to the bathroom. Computers docked his pay when he showed up five minutes late. Computers made sure he got his 2.5 percent bonus if he went to the gym three times a week. Computers didn't care if his knee hurt. Computers sent him animated videos about how to walk faster, how to reach for items more efficiently, how to "optimize his movements."

Computers were what told him what to do and how to do it. That was all he knew about them.

Palmer didn't want to talk to Lilia about that. Who would? About his nothing job, or about the nothing childhood he'd had. About the nothing he still was, when she wasn't around.

So he didn't talk about the warehouse, and she didn't talk about what she did at the university.

Had they talked? All the time. But they had talked about now. About a book one of them was reading. About the feedstreams they watched. She preferred the machine-generated ones. They fascinated her. They taught her everything she needed to know about how to think like a Westerner.

The language models that wrote them were banned in her country. Her government claimed the models were filled with Western biases. In the Federation, they had their own self-censoring, patriotic machines to write stories for their citizens. What were they about? About how to be a good person. The same things the stories here were about, but what it meant to be a good person in her country was different.

Were the stories in her country any good? Yes, they were very good—that was the problem.

Palmer hated machine-generated stories. He sat through them for her sake, but he preferred art house stories—the ones certified machine-language-free, written and brought to the screen only by real people. He didn't care if the subscription to art house feedstreams was more expensive. It was worth it—the machine-generated dramas told a thousand stories, but they all seemed the same.

Then one evening she brought the dioramas home. One for each of them.

A class project, she said. She was working on a new kind of interface. Induced entanglement between neural networks. Wireless human-computer bridges unconstrained by distance, for experimental gaming and bespoke VR feedstreaming. Eventually, you would be able to control what your avatar did in a game with thoughts alone. More than that, even: you would be able to live in the game, like a waking dream.

Palmer often glimpsed Lilia's brilliance, her genius, but that evening he got to see it up close and at length. Her extraordinary mind—

And also the distance between them. He was the kind of

person computers told when to go to the bathroom. She was the kind of person who designed computers that did things no one had ever done before.

But these dioramas were only a prototype. She wanted him to help her beta-test them.

It had been snowing that night—a rare thing even in the coldest winters now. The wet clumps of snow were white in the light of the streetlamps and melted the moment they hit the pavement. He remembered the hiss of the cars passing below.

They sat in front of the dioramas. They weren't impressive. Boxes, square and plain, no larger than the palm of his hand, made of a gray metal, open on one side. Just empty metal boxes. He put on the headset she'd given him—a clumsy-looking 3D-printed crown. Very beta. She put on her own, and they took the pills.

The pills were a mild hallucinogen, she'd explained—they made the neural network more receptive to entanglement. She stroked glyphs across the screen of a school terminal hooked up to the boxes—a big, heavy-looking thing, a terminal of a kind he'd never seen before, and which he never saw again after that night.

He stared into his box as he was told, expecting nothing. The drug started to hit, and he found himself giggling at the silliness of it. At how serious she looked, staring into her own box.

But then a glow appeared in his box. A sheet of color filled the small space, divided itself, resolved into a hillside, a sky, a willow tree—and a young man under the tree, reading a book. It wasn't like a screen—more like a hologram. Fully realized, though—a world that appeared and filled the space inside the box, complete in every detail.

When he leaned in, he could even see the title of the book: *The Little Prince.*

In Lilia's diorama the Thames flowed past Parliament. And on the Thames, a little rowboat. And in that boat, a man and a woman whose faces he could not see, because they were turned away. But he knew it was them, he and Lilia, together.

"What's the game?"

"It's not a game. It's what's inside you. Or—not exactly that. It's like a *translation* of what is inside you. A *state.*"

"How can that be?"

Her pupils were dilated from the pills. When Palmer moved his head the entire room curled like wind through a flag.

"I am still working on finding that out," Lilia said. "But what I want to know is—where am *I* in your diorama?"

"You're the willow tree. And the hill, and the sky. Even the book. It's all you."

In the little studio flat they had shared together, the two dioramas still stood next to one another, in the center of the table.

His diorama now showed a cutaway of an ant farm. Ants walked the sandy tunnels, busily tending eggs and bringing food.

His diorama had been like this for days. He'd even found an ant in it that he believed was him. The Palmer ant. Its thorax was lighter than the others. It walked the same pathways, as busy as the others. But occasionally it paused, lifting its head as if looking or listening beyond the glass. Then, bumped and prodded by the others, it continued on its way.

For weeks, the scene in Lilia's diorama had been the same. In a forest clearing, a girl paced, walking back and forth in front of a dark tree line so thick with trunks there wasn't even room to pass between them. She would walk, then sit, then stand up and walk again. Sometimes she would look up at the sky. That was all.

He had begun to think whatever entanglement might have existed between her and the diorama had been broken. After all, how long could such a thing last, with her so far away? Her diorama was stuck in a loop, maybe. A recording of her last set of feelings before the connection failed.

But now it showed a new scene. She was *in* the forest. It was night, and the thick trunks were all around her. She sat warming her hands at a small fire from which embers rose, floating toward the diorama's boundary.

It's what's inside you. Or—not exactly that. It's like a translation of what is inside you. A state.

Something had changed with her, wherever she was.

She was alive, and something had changed.

That was the message Palmer now typed into his terminal, sending it to the only person who had listened to him for months. His hands shook as he typed:

SOMETHING HAS CHANGED IN HER DIORAMA. SOMETHING MUST HAVE HAPPENED TO HER.

He watched Lilia's avatar warm her hands over the fire. The embers floated so close to the diorama's edge, it seemed they would cross into his world and burn the bare wood of the table.

He held a hand to the diorama as if he might feel the fire's warmth.

His terminal pinged.

STAY THERE. I AM ON MY WAY.

4

THE PRESIDENT / NIKOLAI
The Federation

The President watched Dr. Nikolai Agapov walking toward him.

It was agony, watching people shamble, trapped in their atmosphere of gelatin. It was agony, listening to their voices slur and stagger over words.

The President had not realized, when he insisted on having his thought processes optimized at three times the speed of a standard brain, that it would have this effect.

The President's own movements were slow to him as well, but they had grace and control. By the time he spoke, he had examined the faces of those he spoke to. He had summed up their mood and shaped his response. The words he chose were carefully selected. What did he intend to do with these words? Reassure? Or puncture through their armor like a shaped charge, to the vulnerability underneath?

Others spoke without purpose, simply to speak.

"Good morning, Your Excellency," said Nikolai.

Moaned Nikolai, more like, through the viscous strata of slowed-down time.

The President no longer said good morning to people. He no longer engaged in small talk. It was too painful, listening to them drool out the chopped-up bits of their sentences.

Finally, Nikolai was in front of him. The President turned his attention back to the world. Nikolai rolled up the President's sleeve. He checked the President's pulse at his wrist the old-fashioned way, counting the beats while watching the second hand of his expensive mechanical watch.

Nikolai Agapov was the only human being allowed to touch him. When the President saw that hand approaching his, its freckled skin scattered with dark hair closing in on his own flesh, he always wanted to slap it away. But when the touch came—the fingers pressing on his pulse, the only skin allowed contact with the body of the leader—it felt right.

Perhaps what was wrong with him could be fixed. Perhaps the doctor would have an answer.

But as soon as the President thought these words, he knew they were not true. He had looked in the mirror that morning. He had seen it. Death. It had found him again.

He would have to overcome it. Again.

"So?"

Nikolai could feel the beat of the President's heart, like a whisper against his thumb. He looked up into the President's face, modeled to be close enough to the face that had come before it to inspire a kind of confidence, but not *too close*. Not close enough to call attention to what everyone knew but did not speak of.

When Nikolai had protested that the people would understand what had been done, when one leader spoke and acted so much like the last, Krotov had told him the state was not interested in whether people believed its lies. The state was not looking for plausible deniability. A good lie could always be punctured, with enough work. No, Krotov had said—all they needed was *implausible* deniability. A lie the population would see through immediately but would have to pretend they believed. Even to themselves.

Making themselves believe the bad lie made them complicit. And no one would dare speak the truth. Few would dare even think it.

"And when the West makes their accusations," Krotov said, "we accuse *them* of lying. And we repeat our own lie to them again. Forever."

A cloud of blood vessels had burst scarlet in the white of one of the President's eyes. Where the cloud met the iris, there was an arc of red, as if the iris were separating from the rest of the eye. And there was a pale patch of skin on the President's neck not there during the last examination.

"I need you to take off your shirt."

The President did so.

His right hand, moving toward a button, missed and had to correct its trajectory.

The colorless skin extended halfway down the President's back. There were other scabrous patches. There were flakes of skin along the beltline.

Tests would confirm it, but Nikolai knew what he was looking at: rejection.

"Have you had trouble moving your hand before?"

The President looked down at his own hand.

What was it like, Nikolai wondered, being this man? Being more than a man, but also less?

He hated touching the President. He hated being anywhere near him. He hated being here in the presidential palace, this fake monstrosity of real Italian marble, with its fake Empire chairs in real gold leaf and real silk. He hated returning to the Federation at all.

There had been a time when he had loved the bite of cold as the airport doors opened, the sudden reality of winter between the warm spaces of VIP lounge and VIP car. When he had felt, riding past the bone-legs of birch trees on the outskirts of the capital, as if he were entering the cold core of reality. The *real* world—flakes of sleet whirling like ash against a sunless sky. Watching through the tinted windows of the car as a man let his overbred dog take a steaming shit in a snowbank and walked away without cleaning it up.

He had felt at home here. Here, where every Western brand had its schismatic analogue, its local version just different enough to mark it as "ours" and not "theirs."

He thought he would always feel as if he were returning home when he came back here.

Instead, he felt out of place.

His place was with his family now. His only home was with them. He imagined them at breakfast in Italy, on the cracked terra-cotta tile of the patio. The Italian light. The sun through the trees, the faces of his daughters, who knew nothing of any of this. Who had never lived in the Federation, or even visited it. The concentration on the face of his wife as she cut meat into pieces for their youngest daughter.

But to get back home, to be with them again, he needed to pay attention. He needed to stay awake here. Alert to everything. He had lost that sense of urgency that he needed to survive here. He felt it. He was sleepwalking through his actions, distracted. There was nothing more dangerous.

Wake up.

"It comes and goes," said the President. "What is wrong with me?"

"I will need to do tests."

"And my eye? Can it be repaired?"

"In the short term, we can reduce the appearance. You may have to give video addresses for a few weeks and have the team fix it in postproduction."

"That will be noticed."

"Analysts in the West will capture it," Nikolai said. "But what does that matter? They will tell the foreign agents that we still allow to exist, the so-called journalists, and they will scream at the top of their lungs in the soundproofed digital cells we still allow them to have."

"You are becoming cynical," the President said. "Do not become cynical—a doctor should not be cynical."

Nikolai wished he could be cynical. He was not—when he spoke this way, it was someone else's opinion coming out of his mouth. Cynicism was the only healthy response to the world, but he could not manage it.

Nikolai looked at the President's face. The two unmatched

eyes—one clear, the other marred by its nebula of blood—gazed out the window over the flat, restricted surface of the sea, where no boats were permitted.

Nikolai looked out as well. A white gyre of birds above the shore was all that moved.

Krotov had once joked that even the seagulls needed a permit. That a special unit of the secret police netted them on the beach, examined their papers, and patted them down.

Nikolai almost believed it.

5

NURLAN
The Republic

"I think there are more of them."

"Close the curtain, you idiot. You are showing them where we are."

The UN technocrat let the heavy red curtain fall back into place. What had he called himself? George. He'd said some other name at first. When no one could pronounce it, he said they could call him George. When they couldn't pronounce that either, he just smiled.

"If you want to watch the protest," Atabek continued, "watch it on the screen, like the rest of us. Anyone down there with a rifle scope can see that curtain move. You're lucky they didn't shoot you in the face."

Nurlan watched the scene from a folding chair in the corner of the room. He understood George's urge to pull the curtain aside—to see the protest for himself. He'd had the same urge.

Looking at Atabek's sweating, puffy face, Nurlan was glad he hadn't pulled the curtain aside first. But of course he would not have dared. He would never have drawn attention to himself like that.

A feedscreen taking up an entire wall of the reception hall they were in showed drone footage of the square. A few of the thirty or so MPs who had taken refuge here watched the screen. Others were scattered around the hall, bent over their own terminals. The gold-leaf pseudo-baroque plaster ornament of the room recalled a theater—as if, at any moment, the heavy red curtains would slide aside and the performance would begin.

The sun was down. On the screen, the camera zoomed in, crawling across the crowds outside.

Collecting faces. Matching them against databases. The camera wanted to know the same thing everyone in the room wanted to know: Was this a political protest, or something worse?

All day the protesters had been coming into the square. Never *pouring* in. Never *rushing* in. Just appearing, one group at a time. At 1500 hours an alarm sounded in the parliamentary building. A mechanized voice called for the MPs and their staffers to move to the building's safe areas.

At 1630 or so an MP tried to leave the building, shrugging off the security warnings. He left through a side door but came back with his head bloodied by a cobblestone.

The ambulance that tried to pick him up was beaten back by a hail of stones.

The injured MP, a stained bandage around his skull, now watched the screen with the others.

No one was leaving.

One MP, a woman in a cream-colored suit, had a bright scarf in a national pattern around her throat. Nurlan recognized her as a member of one of the small opposition parties. Asel something. He could not remember her last name or patronymic. When he had first begun to work as a parliamentary staffer, he had known everyone's name. He had memorized all of the MPs. Their names, their party affiliations. But after several years, the information began to seem meaningless. What did it matter who they were? They came and went, or stayed. They argued incessantly, and not a single one of them had ever done anything worth remembering in all the time he had worked here. Eventually, they became a same-like, meaningless political blur.

"I don't like the look of them," Asel said to George. "They are not from the city."

"How can you tell that?" George asked. The UN technocrat had sunk into one of the deep leather couches along one wall of the room. He looked frightened.

He was right to be frightened. Nurlan looked around at the tense, meaty faces of the MPs in the hall. There were MPs from parties that would not be caught dead together outside a parliamentary session. The fact that they were willing to be in the same room together, outside of session, was cause for alarm.

Something terrible was going to happen. Everyone in the room could feel it.

"I can tell by the way they are dressed," the cream-suited woman said. "And they are all men. In the morning, there were both women and men holding signs on the square.

"Those were real protesters. They were dressed differently. They were local as well. They were chanting, shouting, singing. But once these men started to show up, those real protesters melted away. These men were bused in. They have been paid to be here."

"But by who?" George asked.

Atabek stabbed a thick finger at George. "You! You have a direct line to the Prime Minister. Tell the Prime Minister to fix this."

"Fix what?" someone shouted from across the room. "The subsidized energy prices dragging our country down? The Prime Minister *is* fixing it. Shock therapy. The PM knows that's what's needed. People need to learn to conserve. To turn their lights off, that's all."

"I'll turn your fucking lights off!" Atabek yelled.

"I'd like to see you try."

Someone laughed. Atabek swiveled his head, trying to figure out who it was.

Asel addressed herself to George, ignoring Atabek.

"They aren't chanting anything, see? They aren't doing anything at all. They are standing around, waiting."

"Waiting for what?" asked George.

"For the rest to show up. For their orders."

"Where are the riot police?" Atabek said. "Ask the PM where the *police* are. There should be buses full of them here by now. They could clear this square in a few minutes. We could all go home. A couple of snipers on the building could do it even faster . . ."

"A few hours of standing around waiting, and Atabek's already calling for blood," someone said.

Across the room, a group of MPs were sitting at one of the meeting tables, watching their terminals. "For God's sake," one of them said. This was Jyldyz Kadyrova, a center-right MP.

"What?" Atabek asked.

"The Prime Minister has doubled energy prices *again*."

"Madness!"

"None of us are going home," someone said.

"You get the Prime Minister on your terminal," Atabek said to George, standing over him now, "and ask him if he has lost his mind. What is he trying to do?"

"Here," George said, handing a handheld subterminal to Atabek. "Ask the PM yourself."

Outside, there was shouting. On the screen, the drone footage showed a mass of men against the metal fence now, several of them hanging from the bars. Security footage in a split screen zoomed in on angry faces.

"It's a provocation," Kadyrova said. "A provocation, plain and simple. Our enemies . . ."

"Our enemies?" This was Erlis Jeenbaev, a "graybeard"—the great-grandson of one of the Republic's last communists. "A provocation? You pushed for energy price increases for years. You called our citizens 'parasites.' You called them 'red commie beetles subsisting on the dung of international assistance.' You said it was 'time to join the free world, and to find out nothing is free.'"

"What did you do, write it all down? I'm flattered. I thought you spent most of your time in Parliament napping. At least my speeches kept you awake." Kadyrova looked around with a grin, hoping for a laugh. But no one was listening to her.

"It's called *having a memory*," Jeenbaev said. "An inconvenience in politics, and something you, conveniently, are not burdened by. You were warned increases in energy costs would cause instability, and you kept at it."

"The World Bank—"

"It's not about the *World Bank*. It's about the corrupt businesspeople you want to sell our republic's national interests off to. It's about lining your pockets."

"I never suggested *this*. I never suggested we do it all in a single *day*. This price increase is sabotage." She pointed a finger at George. "Ask *him* what we should do. This is *their* fault. We're nothing but an experiment to these bastards. And the assembly *voted* for rationalization. All of you. You wanted this. Now look what we get . . ."

"You have forgotten your own vote, Ms. Kadyrova."

"I was absent that day! I was ill!"

"You lobbied others to vote for rationalization. Then—like a coward—you stayed home. Your intention was clear enough. Your coalition gave the PM the supermajority needed."

"It's an experiment the UN is running," said Jyldyz. "I'm sure of it. They've been experimenting on our republic from the start! We're convenient to them—not a part of the EU, not a powerful country like the US. We're small, and poor. A safe place for them to play their games. The only country that will get annoyed if we fall apart on their flanks is the Federation. In fact, maybe that's the point—to turn us into a thorn in the Federation's side. And when the Federation invades us? Who will be there to protect us? The EU? The UN? None of them. That's what I'm saying. It's a provocation—they want to—"

"Will you shut up with your nonsense conspiracies?" Atabek shouted at her. "I am trying to get some answers!"

She glared at him but was quiet.

"Yes, Prime Minister," Atabek said into the subterminal at his ear. "Yes, a question. I want to know if you are aware of what is happening here. On the square. They are gathering—more and more of them every hour. It is just a matter of time before—"

He was silent for a moment.

All I want, Nurlan thought, *is to go home. To be in my apartment, alone. To turn on the feedscreen and let this day, which started out like any other day, end like any other day—with forgetting what had happened, with drifting off to a comedy feed, with some decent food delivered to my door. That, and a bit of daydreaming about Hazal. Holding the thought of her in my mind for a few minutes. Thinking of when we will finally meet.*

Nothing else. I haven't ever asked for anything else.

"But . . . Yes, I understand. But . . . at the very least—"

Atabek stood for several seconds with the subterminal at his ear. Nurlan watched his face as it went slack. Atabek stared at the thick red curtains, as if he could see the massing crowd through them.

The screen showed the men on the square building a bonfire. A hot white space at the center of the drone images, like a hole stabbed through the pixels. Every time a camera panned across it, the screen flared.

Atabek handed the subterminal to George and sat down, saying nothing.

"What did the PM say?" the woman in the cream-colored suit asked.

Atabek passed a hand over his face. "The Prime Minister said energy prices will double again in one hour."

Home suddenly seemed very far away.

Nurlan's terminal vibrated.

WHERE ARE YOU?

6

LILIA
The Federation

Lilia lay in the back of the Niva, in the cramped foot space between the back bench and the small four-by-four's front passenger seat. Most of the time she lay face down, with the hump in the center of the floor pressed against her stomach, listening to the whine of the transmission through the vehicle's rubber-matted floor.

Everything hurt. She rolled onto her side to relieve her muscles, but in that position the hump in the floor dug into her ribs. Soon she had to shift again, curling into a ball, with her legs on the hump and her back against the interior side panel.

The ancient Niva had been human-driven when it was manufactured. Its aftermarket autodrive was jerky and inaccurate, self-correcting to tug itself back into its lane every few moments, shifting late, after the engine had revved too far. The autodrive was a gray-painted box half the size of a person, welded into place against the dashboard of the car where the steering wheel, driver's seat, shifter, and pedals used to be. Twice, Lilia had banged her head against its corners.

There had been a note on the seat telling her to get into the cramped back seat area and keep her head down. There she found minimal comforts: a glass one-liter bottle of water, several military nutrition bars, a plastidown blanket.

As the Niva crawled through city traffic she was sure she would be discovered. Someone would yank the door open. She would be pulled from the car. They would beat her in the street, as they still did sometimes, to demonstrate to other "citizens" that the state did not limit itself to controlling its citizens only through technology. There was plenty the state could do with tech, but it could also choose to beat you to death the old-fashioned way.

Her fear of discovery, her fear of being caught and beaten, of being imprisoned and executed, was so intense that it was nauseating. What had she done? How had she dared attempt this escape?

Although she had been hungry in the morning, it was not until long after the Niva had left the city that she could bring herself to attempt eating one of the nutrition bars.

It tasted like compacted sawdust and something sweet—raisins, maybe—passed through a greasy industrial process. She kept it down.

At one point the Niva pulled over and jerked to a halt. The door was tugged open.

Lilia knew, then, that she was dead. The Niva had stopped in a construction site: the forest torn away, piles of raw logs, bark wounded by bulldozer blades, roots clotted with mud. In one pile were the gingerbread window and ripped eaves of an ancient izba, the crushed whitewash of a dead family hearth. Machinery groaned in front of the skeleton of a high-rise.

A terrible place to die.

But where would be a good place to die?

A man in a hard hat leaned down over her.

"Please," she said, her hands up as if it might be possible to defend herself from what came next.

"Good. You're alive."

Before Lilia could respond, the man tossed a bag into the back seat and slammed the door.

In the bag were more bottles of water, more terrible nutrition bars. A note read: "Soon."

Three or four hours into its drive, the Niva lurched off the road, into the forest itself. It crawled along a rutted track that threw her head and back against the interior panels of the car and bounced her so hard against the hump in the floor that she was sure it would leave bruises. Another hour went by, and another, and another.

Finally, she could not lie down anymore. She raised her head far enough to peer out the window. The pale light of summer evening came through the trees. There were denuded spears of drowned cedars everywhere, killed by the smear of bog water pooled at their roots, green in the half-light. Fallen trees tangled with those still standing.

The road—though you could barely call it that—threaded a trace of higher ground. It was muddy but still passable, though the Niva's wheels slipped and slid. She sat up.

The bog would spread. It would take this road as well soon. And if it had already done so? What if all of this ended with the Niva sliding off into the water? With her dying out here, drowned in some endless bog? Or wandering until she starved?

There was so much she would be able to do with a terminal in front of her. With access to a network and the tools she was used to.

Those forests—the electronic forests of interconnected data—were the ones she knew. The forests behind the screen, where the networks of roots and fungal systems were digital. Hidden connectivities, linking everything. Where she could be anywhere in the world in moments, could do anything she set her mind to. Where she had done things no one else had done. Where she was no helpless passenger. Where she was a creator, able to reshape the forest itself. To bend its connections to her will. To fold the space between things until two far-off points touched, and walk across that fold from one place to another.

But here, in the horizonless world of the real forest, all she could do was die.

The Niva passed a hunter's shack, its slack walls rotting into the bog's green-gray waters. She did not lie down again. It hurt too much, and what was the point? There was no one out here.

She sat in the back seat, watching the trees crawl past as the Niva lurched up onto higher, sandier ground.

She had lived her whole life surrounded by the taiga. But she had never entered it. In fact, she didn't know *anyone* who went into the trees.

That was strange, wasn't it? This forest stretched, unbroken, across a third of the earth. Across an entire continent.

There were parts of it, still, where no human foot had trod. But her whole life, she had ignored its existence.

How could you ignore a thing as vast as this?

But all the people in the cities ignored the taiga. Lilia used to see those they called "forest people" when they strayed into town. They were strangers, as foreign as if they had traveled in from another country. Berry gatherers, mushroom collectors, hunters, trappers, mad religious hermits, people who had lost everything and walked away.

You saw them at a bus stop with a walking stick and a stained coat, wearing a backpack gone shapeless with use. They were as out of place in the cities as she now felt here.

We all have places where we belong. And places where we do not.

She had believed her place was in London. She had convinced herself that she was meant to be there, not here. That all along, her life had been leading there.

Because she was too good for this place, right? Too good for this country. Too good for the ugly concrete prefab buildings. Too good for her dreary local university stinking of mop water and bad pipes. Too good to keep saying the things she needed to say to stay safe. Too good to make the compromises she needed to make in order to survive here.

That was what her father had believed about her. That was what *she* had come to believe about herself.

When she got the offer from London, she never expected the Federation would let her leave.

But then they gave her the exit visa. When they handed it over to her, they took her into a back room in the special issuance office. There, a man in uniform sat at a battered desk, under a picture of the President.

"So, you think you are too good for us, is that it?" he said. As if he had seen right into her mind.

She could hear the pounding of her own heart. She answered, "No."

"Well," he said, stamping the exit visa into her passport with an ancient self-inking stamp, "you will have two years to find out. If you decide you are too good for us, you can apply for asylum there—"

"I don't—"

He held up a hand. "And they might give it to you. And we might let you have it. Or we might send someone to take you back. Or . . ."

And now she looked at his face. At his war-burned and reconstructed face. Which of their country's many wars against its neighbors had done this to him? Lab-grown skin, pink and youthful and unlined, but as false as a mask. His aged, inflamed eyes looked out from behind it.

". . . you may come back on your own. I have been there. To the West. It is wonderful—and empty. I think someone like you will come back. You'll enjoy yourself until you find out *enjoying yourself* is all there is to do there. For people from here—for people like you and me—that is never enough. We'll be seeing you again."

Had he been right? Had she come back here because she *needed* this place? Because it had been too *easy* there, and easy wasn't enough?

No. In London, she had been free for the first time, and

had seen what that meant: At the university, she had finally been able to do the things she had only thought of doing, planned and schemed about back home. The ideas she had filled her notebooks with, the tests she had laboriously carried out, pushing up against the inferior capacities of terminals at work and school, were finally in reach. She had been able, there, to do things no one else had done. She had met a man she loved and had conversations with him without fear, talking about things as if nothing could touch them.

She wished, now, that she and Palmer had talked about even more. That she had been able to tell him about this place, about the terror of it. But she had thought that there was time for those conversations, and no rush.

He was wrong, the war-scarred man in the back room who stamped her exit visa. She had found meaning there, had seen what life could be like—what a life of accomplishment might look like.

She had no need to suffer. She had no masochistic need to scrape for survival here in the Federation's closed, suffocating system. She had come back for a simple reason—she had come back to say goodbye to the one person in the world who had been there for her when no one else was. Who had cared for her when no one else would. Without doing that, she had known she couldn't be fully present in her new life. And she owed it to her father—to tell him that this time, when she left, it would be forever.

The Niva came to a stop in a small clearing.

The car's engine ticked.

What had she imagined would be waiting for her here? An airfield? A drone pad from which some hexcopter would lift her into the air and away from all of this? Baba Yaga's chicken-legged fucking *hut*?

There was nothing but the hungry buzz of the millions of mosquitoes waiting outside the glass.

Then a branch snapped. The treetops shuddered.

Something enormous was moving toward her through the trees.

7

NIKOLAI
The Federation

"All I need from you, Nikolai," said Krotov, "is an assessment. You see the signs. How long does he have?"

It was late morning. They sat at a small table in the sun-flecked yard of Krotov's Faraday-caged dacha, a mile away from the President's palace. They sat at the center of onion layers of security. Nothing here was electronic. Krotov wore an analog watch, its skeleton face filled with exposed gears, its transparency a demonstration of its harmlessness.

Even the watch made Nikolai suspicious. *Do you know what your descendants will be capable of?*

But Nikolai was drifting, seeing his other life as if through a window opened in the world between himself and Krotov's hated face across the table.

The cracked terra-cotta tile of the patio. The sun through the trees, the faces of his girls, who knew nothing of any of this.

Would he return to it again?

Not if he didn't pay attention. He couldn't afford to daydream here. Not in this country. Not sitting across from Krotov, officially head of the "Investigative Committee"—but in reality, the head of the Federation's entire security apparatus.

Krotov was famous for his stories. Storytelling was a weapon for him. He used it to probe an opponent's weaknesses, size up an ally's loyalties, uncover a plot. Someone once said, "Krotov will talk you to sleep. And you'll wake up on your knees in the taiga with the barrel of a gun pressed to your neck."

The man who had said those words was dead. He'd died in a one-car crash on a road he'd never traveled before. A road he'd had no reason to be on.

It was the kind of death that sent a message.

That wasn't the only story about Krotov. There were so many others. There was a story that Krotov had once whispered in a man's ear, and the man had gone home and shot himself.

Wake up.

"Less than three months," Nikolai said, thinking of the burst blood vessels in the President's eye, the flaking skin down to the beltline.

The eye worried him, but the skin worried him more. He had seen the skin of a blank's entire hand come off like a glove, right down to necrotizing muscle and bone beneath.

"Why is it happening?" Krotov stabbed an eggplant roll. He turned it on his fork to keep the olive oil from dripping and placed it between his lips.

"Rejection."

"This didn't happen to the previous iteration. We had a good run with that one. Fifteen years until the *assassination*."

His stress on the word "assassination" highlighted what they both understood: it had been planned, an act of convenience that allowed the purge of the last surviving charities, journalists, and artists critical of the state.

Nikolai remembered that day—the President in the transfer room, naked, his face still spattered with fake blood.

"Tell me it won't hurt, Nikolai."

"It won't hurt. You will go to sleep and wake up younger, that's all." He had glanced over at the blank waiting in its sterile, transparent coffin. "And better looking."

"What a world, Nikolai," the President had said. "No old age, no sickness, and no death. Finally we can have both our wisdom and our health."

The President said *we*—but it was only *he* who could have those things. It was only *he* who could escape old age, sickness, and death.

But there was a flash of agony when they placed the crown on his head. And though the President's neural pattern transferred perfectly, Nikolai wondered if people were more than that pattern. He wondered if there was something that did not survive these transfers. Something that died with the flesh.

The new President campaigned against half a dozen scarecrows from the official opposition parties. People suspected. But they did nothing.

"It could have been caused by the modifications that were requested," Nikolai said to Krotov. "There aren't enough blanks to do a study. We don't know anything except what we have seen and done so far. We know X works or Y does not. But most of the time, we can't say what the reasons are."

Krotov leaned back in his chair and tilted his face upward, his eyes closed. The clean, vulnerable throat, the red fleck of a razor nick on his Adam's apple, the coin of sun through the trees that marked a place where a bullet could end him.

Then what? Free elections?

Why not? Why not free elections?

But in his mind, he saw the mob, the smoking rocket holes in the face of a government building, the fires.

There was always the mob.

There was always Krotov too. You didn't need to copy Krotov's mind. It copied itself. Krotov was fungal. He spread underground, attaching himself to the country's root systems, trading information for nutrients. Krotov's mind wasn't in his skull: it was diffused in the soil. This thing in front of Nikolai called "Krotov" was nothing but a poisonous mushroom pushed up from the forest floor, born of the mycelium of violence woven through the dirt.

All I want is to go home.

That was the most dangerous thing. His thoughts of his family intruding. Distracting him from what was in front of him.

Eventually, he would make a mistake.

Wake up.

"You are tired. I am tired too, Nikolai," Krotov said, not opening his eyes, his face still tilted upward to the sky. "All we want is peace. Instead, we get this. All I do is cover up the mistakes of others."

Was he speaking of Nikolai? Did he think the President's sickness was somehow Nikolai's fault?

As if Krotov sensed the thought, tasted it in the networked ichor that threaded him into everything, he said, "I don't blame you. I blame the President himself. He wanted improvements made. He wanted to think faster than the rest of us. He reached too far. And that's just it. The overreaching, the mistakes"—he tilted his face back down and met Nikolai's blank, waiting gaze—"which always lead to more mistakes. This country is nothing but mistakes. Have you heard the story of Kolpashevsky Yar?"

"I have not," Nikolai said. And he prepared himself. He had to understand the story—had to understand, more importantly, *why* it was being told to him.

"It is a sandy bank of the Ob River, near Tomsk. There was a prison there, in the 1930s. So many people to shoot back then. Into the pit of the prison yard the dead went. When one mass grave was full, they dug another. And another.

"Decades later, in 1979, a spring flood washed the bank away, exposing the corpses. The pits had been limed to keep the smell down, but the lime had also preserved the victims. The purged, the suppressed. People who had not only been killed but eliminated from our history. People who had been painted out of photographs, edited out of encyclopedia entries. Vanished commissars, rising from their graves. You could still recognize some of their faces.

"Of course, their relatives came, looking for their loved ones. So the secret police blocked access to the river. They brought in river ferries and used the wash from their propellers to churn up the banks, to chew away at the rest of the graves. Then they sent out 'sanitary crews' to tie scrap metal to the corpses and sink them in the river. The sanitary crews were made up of whoever the secret police could press-gang into the filthy job. Some had relatives in those pits . . ."

He paused, mopping up oil from his plate with a piece of bread. "People talk about the pain of the descendants, seeing their relatives murdered all over again. But what I think of is the local secret police. I think of the men sent in from the capital to supervise the whole mess. How humiliating! The bumbling stupidity of it. The embarrassment.

"It was a mistake, shooting so many people. We know that now. They knew it then. In the early days, they shot people for being Polish, for being engineers, for having a grandfather with a title. They shot people for nothing at all, just to make their quotas. The joke back then was that the secret police would shoot you for being left-handed—twice!

"Then, generations later, some poor fool finds himself tying scrap metal to corpses. He has to go up and down the Ob River hunting for the corpses that might have drifted away. He has to give people idiotic explanations he knows they won't believe about 'sanitary measures.' And for what? To conceal the incompetence of his predecessors.

"The public thinks these men are evil. Men who covered up crimes the state should have answered for. The state! Ridiculous. There *is* no state. There are only *people*. The 'state' is nothing more than people like you and me, trying to make the best of the worst. We bury and rebury the bodies, but there are always more corpses. And there is always some miserable asshole with a shovel, trying to dig up his grandfather's skull to wail over it. Which reminds me of another joke—but I'll tell you that one later. I'll save it for after we are done with what we need to do."

"What is it we need to do?" Nikolai asked.

Krotov wiped the imported, high-end virgin olive oil from his mouth with a napkin so white it made Nikolai's irises contract.

"We need to make a new President. But we need to get it *right* this time. No more mistakes. Of course, we will have to create a few more corpses—not too many, I hope—for our descendants to deal with. But don't worry, Nikolai. I'll make the corpses. All you have to do is be a doctor. And report back to me, as you always have."

8

ELMIRA / PALMER
The Union

Elmira rolled the wasp's controller in her palm. The insect settled on the window glass. The light of a passing ambulance pulsed red on the metallic fibers of its wings as it crawled across the pane. Elmira squeezed the controller. The wasp stopped moving. She drew a pair of tongs from a pocket and plucked it from the glass. As she lifted the wasp from the pane its wings retracted into its body. She placed it in a chromium cylinder and slipped it into her pocket.

The faint outlines of the dioramas' edges were stamped into the table's cheap finish. Elmira could sense that other things had also been moved from their places.

The apartment had been abandoned in haste.

A small voice asked a question in her ear.

"He's gone," she said. She placed her terminal on the table and swiped at the screen.

"No. I used the callbox downstairs. There was no answer, so I bypassed the security on the entryway terminal and knocked at his apartment door. No answer there either, so I forced the e-lock. He's gone."

The voice hissed another question.

"Of course I didn't expect him to leave. *He* is the one who contacted *me*. And yes, the dioramas are gone as well." She swiped right at the screen, swiped left, paused. Enlarged something.

"Facerec picked him up on a public security camera leaving the building twenty minutes ago. But there's an observation shadow in the alleyway. I'm scrolling feeds. I don't pick him up again, so unless he's standing in the alley . . ."

She waited while the voice hissed in her ear.

"Facerec has scanned the cameras in a fifty-K radius and picked up nothing. There is no way he could leapfrog that many cameras."

Again, the tinny hiss. Elmira clenched and unclenched her left hand, massaged her palm.

"Of course. I've been running choicerec since long before I walked into this room. And of course . . ." She paused, listened. "I'm looking at his terminal now. He left it on the windowsill. Choicerec maps him as almost never having had his terminal more than one to two meters from his body in the last six months. So there has been an intervention."

She walked across the room, picked up Palmer's terminal from the windowsill, scrolled back through the message log.

STAY THERE. I AM ON MY WAY.

"The last message is from me. They contacted him some other way. And he doesn't have his terminal, which means I don't think choicerec will help us, for now. They'll be jamming his pattern. They won't let him make his own choices."

She looked out into the street. The street would be looking back, of course. Whoever it was that had taken Palmer from her, she was sure they had dug into the city feed or opened an eye of their own on the scene, framing her in the window, knowing they had her beat, for now.

That was what *she* would be doing if she were them: watching this window.

She raised her hand and waved. *You got me. For now, anyway.*

"Maybe," she said. "But I think they are moving *him*, too..."

She waited for the chattering in her ear to trail off.

"He's the other end of the neural entanglement. They'll want to keep him alive, see how it works. See if they can reverse engineer it... That will be easier with him alive."

She slipped his terminal into a Faraday bag.

"Until he drops whatever they're using to mask him. Or until they stop making choices for him long enough for his choicerec pattern to emerge somewhere. If I had to bet, I'd say choicerec will pick him up before facerec does. He might be clever enough to keep whatever mask they have him using on, as long as they remind him to do it—but we've mapped his terminal. His personal patterns are obvious. We'll pick him up eventually. All he has to do is select something, and one of our crawlers will identify him."

She began a slow walk around the room, examining the windowsill, the walls, the furniture, all the objects of an abandoned life.

"Maybe," she said, watching an autoframe on a side table run through a slideshow of Palmer and Lilia together, smiling into terminal lenses across Europe, one tourist backdrop after another behind them. "But I haven't lost one yet. I don't think he'll be my first."

Palmer woke up not knowing who or where he was.

It was a familiar feeling. After working a double or triple shift at the warehouse, he would collapse into a sleep so deep he lost his sense of place. And, if he was tired enough, his sense of who he was.

He felt the rocking, the rhythm of the rails, and remembered. The blind was drawn. He pushed the plastidown train blanket off. Through a gap between windowsill and blind, countryside slashed past the high-speed train: grain field, copse, house, crossroads, pond.

He had been no one for a moment, on waking up.

Palmer Blank.

That was what they had called him at school. Some girl on the swim team who hated him for an obscure school reason had come up with it.

"Palmer *Blank*. Because he's no one. Whoever he's with, that's who he is."

Why? He'd never been any more of a conformist than anyone else—than that girl, for example. All that was left of her in his memory was an angle of dark hair. Tan arms across the coping of the pool. What set *her* apart from anyone else? What set anyone apart?

But the name had stuck. Palmer Blank. He even said it accidentally, sometimes. Blank . . . I mean, Blake.

But he really *didn't* know where he was, this time.

Or even who he was—or who they were pretending he was now.

He had slept in the hat they told him to wear at all times, the hat he took from a paper bag in a trash can in the alley next to his apartment building, as instructed. It was a sort of watch cap—black, knit of some breathable material.

His instructions had been clear enough. The drone—a thing like a large, suction-cup-legged beetle that had landed on his window, had pressed its thorax against the glass. The thorax flattened into a screen, and flashed the instructions in sequence:

THEY ARE COMING TO KILL YOU

GET OUT NOW

GO TO ALLEY

FIRST BLUE BIN RIGHT HAND SIDE

PAPER BAG

TAKE HAT

TAKE TERMINAL

KEEP HAT ON AT ALL TIMES

TERMINAL HAS TICKET FOR TRAIN

TAKE DIORAMAS

NOTHING ELSE

GET OUT NOW

NOW

NOW

And he had obeyed.

He should be frightened. Terrified. What did he feel instead? Relief? Maybe. At least something was happening now. At least something was moving, after months of stasis.

The countryside rushed past, repeating the same objects, alternating a sequence.

He recalled the first time he had traveled, during a three-month period of mandated unemployment—his "cyclical sabbatical," as the government termed their scheme for reducing joblessness. A "paycation," as everyone else called it. Laid off with benefits to keep the unemployment numbers down.

Before that first paycation, Palmer had thought life was different elsewhere.

It wasn't. It was just carried out in a different language. All the countries he traveled to had gone over to rationalization. The entire EU had done it. The UK, most of the Commonwealth. The North American Union, the Central and South American Economic Unions. Rationalization had spread to countries in the Middle East, in Africa, in Central Asia.

In the city centers Palmer had traveled to, things looked different—there were cathedrals, castles built on patterns one did not see elsewhere, temples. But the back end of human reality was repetition. The countryside was the same everywhere. The edges of the cities were the same too: age-sagged warehouses with broken windows, wastes of rails in the switching yards, silent cranes, loading docks and trucks.

In every country he saw people going to work with expressionless faces, coming home from work with the same faces, slack with exhaustion.

Lilia had asked him once if things were better after

rationalization. This wasn't a question he had ever asked himself. He had never thought about it. He was too young, maybe, to make a proper comparison. But before rationalization everything was nearing collapse. That was what people said, anyway. Protests, labor shortages, supply chain breakdowns, strikes, wars, the climate catastrophe no one seemed to have the will to deal with—a constant cycle of disasters.

Things must have been bad before rationalization, he told Lilia—but that wasn't why rationalization happened. Or, at least, it didn't seem like why.

What brought it all on was the Paris dirty bomb.

He had been in year one. He didn't remember being afraid: it was worse than that.

It was the *adults* who were afraid.

He remembered his father taping plastic sheeting over the windows. He remembered his mother's shaking hands. On the television, images of the radioactive cloud drifting over continental Europe. Inching its way toward the channel.

Then the mass arrests in the Paris banlieues. The trials, the pogroms against immigrant communities all over Europe. In London, council housing apartment blocks burned.

But what he remembered most was his evacuation to the countryside. How he had lived a month there with a foster family. Little splinters of that time. A train platform filled with children. A muddy field. A hike along a crest, with piles of rock like ruined castles. His foster mother's hands, gnarled by work and early arthritis, though her face was still young. His big, kind foster father, now reduced by faulty memory to Wellington boots and a corduroy jacket out at the elbows. A pig steaming in the cold morning as it rooted in a trough.

He hadn't been afraid. He remembered it as an adventure: one of the best months of his childhood. "Strange memories to have of a disaster," he'd said to Lilia.

"No—it's not strange. I remember being in an organization called the Young Guard. It was indoctrination into our system—propaganda about the terrors of the West, loyalty oaths, marching—but all I really remember is a trip to the mountains and how much I loved the color of my Young Guard scarf. I thought it made me look important. Serious. We were just little boys and girls. It was a part of our life, that's all. And that's how we end up with nostalgia even for the awful things. That's childhood."

"I didn't do it, but I wish I had," one of the dirty bomb defendants had said. No more than a boy himself. "I wish I had done it, and worse. You deserve it. Every one of you."

They played that over and over again while immigrant communities across Europe burned.

And then the conspiracy was uncovered. The bombing was an inside job. The work of radical right-wing elements so intent on sowing fear that they were willing to destroy their own cities and murder their own people to do it. And it wasn't immigrant kids going to prison anymore—it was government officials. Parliamentarians, police.

He remembered a woman on the living room feedscreen talking about "a fundamental lack of faith in government and in our institutions."

A lack of faith that spread from Paris outward like the dirty bomb's radioactive cloud.

"I meant what I said," the boy from the banlieue said when

he was exonerated. "I mean it even more now. I wish I had done it, and worse."

The first referendum for rationalization was close. Palmer remembered the protests, when the police, under PM orders, had laid down their shields and walked away. The protesters had scaled a fence or two, set fire to a few cars. But then—when there was no one standing in front of them, no wall of riot police shoving them back, nothing to resist, they had milled around and then simply—dissipated.

In other countries, referendums passed by wider margins. Wider and wider, when they saw how calm descended on countries once a PM took over.

Then it became inevitable. Everyone would rationalize. The incentives were right. It was easier: all their parliaments had to do under rationalization was busy themselves with bureaucratic details while the artificial minds of the Prime Ministers made the big decisions. The human parliaments got to tout the results—the minimum-wage increases, the social safety net improvements, the economic stabilization, the CEO pay caps, the pension funds that didn't get raided or collapse.

They got to take the credit for near-zero unemployment, guaranteed housing, affordable mortgages, better mental health, cleaner streets . . . and without rationalization, you couldn't compete with the other countries and their smoothly running economies, their social benefits. It was either rationalize or lose out.

Was it better? Yes, he'd told Lilia finally. It was better.

But the question nagged him. If everything was better

now, why did it feel as if nothing had changed—as if the system that existed before rationalization hadn't gone away? As if, instead, it had been cemented into place? Made more comfortable for the people at the bottom—but also made permanent, so that they would *always* be at the bottom?

They said each PM was attuned to the "lifeways" of the country it managed. That what the PM sought was the ideal expression of those lifeways. "A bespoke, national solution for human thriving," as the public service announcements repeated.

Maybe that was the problem. Maybe the problem wasn't the PMs—maybe it was the material fed into them to begin with. *Maybe our lifeways are shit,* Palmer thought, *and feeding our shitty ideas into some new kind of intelligence was never going to turn them into anything but reprocessed shit.*

He never said that to her. He didn't know how to tell that to someone for whom things back home were so much worse. It sounded ridiculous. It *was* ridiculous, complaining to her about his comfortable, safe life. After all she'd had to overcome to get here. And anyway—if he'd hardly thought about any of it before meeting her, could it be that bad?

The Palmer Blake ant in his diorama, lifting its head as if it heard or saw something beyond the glass. Asking a question. Then, prodded by the others, continuing on its way.

That was him—knowing there was something wrong, asking a question, but doing nothing.

Wasn't that everyone, though?

What was the scene in his diorama now? Palmer wanted to look, to take the boxes out of his bag, but knew he should not. The dioramas, after all, were what *they* were after.

He touched the fabric of the hat. He knew it altered his face for the facerec cameras, because when he had been scanned for boarding the facerec blinked green. They wouldn't have paired the ticket to *his* face—that would have logged his destination.

The hat changed him, somehow.

On his way to the train station he had seen so many cameras. Hundreds of them. The cameras had always been there, of course. But he'd never noticed how many there were. And those were just the visible ones—on the eaves of buildings, on lampposts and cornices.

It wasn't quite true to say he'd never noticed the cameras before. It was that they had always been unimportant to him—a part of the background like the buildings they hung on. He'd never thought of the fact that they were *looking*—watching, searching for people. And now, perhaps, for him.

The terminal they had given him, the one he had dug out from the paper bag in the trash can, was an old model. Its choice assistant and biometric recognition systems were disabled. There was a password taped to the back, then a prompt to change that password the first time he logged in. No apps, no apparent connectivity: the thing was little more than a brick. And heavy. It had one of those batteries that lasted for weeks and an industrial case you could hit with a car. The kind of terminal construction workers might carry around on site. Or shift supervisors at the warehouse. Single purpose, firewalled off so it couldn't be used to waste time. To "steal" time, as the companies always put it.

Why had he trusted these people? Not even "these people," in fact, but a drone that landed on his window?

Maybe because when that last NOW flashed across the thing's thorax, he thought back to the room where the woman interviewed him. The salvaged-looking furniture. The heavy green metal desk, the old-fashioned lamp with its cord running to a socket in the wrong place on the wall. Nothing but a folding chair for him to sit in. Rectangular shadows of grime where frames had once hung. He saw her in that high-backed leather chair, folding her hands on the desk, smiling at him, and saying: "Tell me your story."

It was all wrong. *They* had contacted *him*. And he had gone, fool that he was, thinking they were the spy-vs.-spy people he was finally being allowed to speak to, the kind of people who might be able to *do* something about what had happened to Lilia.

But why had he believed that? They could be anyone. They could be—and were, most likely—Federation agents mopping up. Looking for the dioramas, for other traces of her. Covering up their crime.

Or hunting for her, still. She might have gotten away from them, and they were trying to get a lead on where she was now.

With that thorax scrolling its red NOW across the pane of his window, he had realized: it was all wrong. The furniture assembled into the ghost of an office, the bleak hallway—it was the thinnest of stage sets, built to fool him into telling his story.

And, being a fool, he had fallen for it.

But he wouldn't have fallen for it today. Between then and now, his perspective on the world had changed. He'd woken up. Now the trap was clear to him.

He looked at the backpack containing the dioramas. He

had looped the straps through a handle on the compartment wall and tied them together.

He wouldn't take the dioramas out, but he did take out the book. Lilia's book.

He'd grabbed it impulsively. He had an idea that, somehow, on the other side of all of this, he would hand it to her.

It was the book she had bought at the airport. The forbidden book, the death sentence in her country that anywhere else was nothing but words on pages: *The Forever Argument*.

He opened it to a random page in the middle. Here, Lilia had underlined a passage:

From that moment, we understood that the state was everywhere. The state did not need to anticipate us: it was always with us. It shaped the mistakes we would make, and it was there to take us into its prisons when we made them.

He ran a finger over the page. He could feel the indentation, the weight of her pen stroke as she'd underlined.

Someone tried the door of his compartment. Rattled the handle.

He looked up at the shadow behind pebbled glass.

Already.

But then he heard a laugh in the corridor, and the shadow slid away. Just someone trying the wrong door.

He looked at the thumb latch on the train compartment door. Nothing was safe. There must be a passkey that would turn it. And if there was a passkey, copies could be made.

There was always someone with the key to the locked door, someone watching through the eye of a camera, someone listening on a terminal.

And he did not know who was helping him. And he did not know why.

Once, at the warehouse, he stepped out from an aisle and an automated heavypicker the size of a bus whipped past his face, so close it caught the toe of his work boot and smeared the boot's outsole on the warehouse floor, leaving a smudge like a child's melted black crayon.

Death had been that close to him yesterday as well. He felt it.

But he knew more today than he had yesterday. He was learning fast.

9

NURLAN
The Republic

WHERE ARE YOU?
Hazal's message blinked on the screen.
Nurlan typed into his terminal:
YOU WOULD NEVER BELIEVE ME
"Five revolutions in three generations, a parliament that never could agree on anything," Asel said. She was now sitting next to the man who called himself George. "My father used to tell a story: Once upon a time our people all lived as farmers. They tilled the fields. They tended their animals. For many years there was no famine and no war. Then one day, they had a meeting in the village assembly hall. They argued for days—about everything. The sizes of their fields, the soil, their rights to well water, the livestock this one had or that one didn't have. It turned out none of them were happy. So, for the first and only time, they voted unanimously to solve the problem."

She was one of those who were most comfortable when they were talking. That was when *she* was safe. Her face grew calm as she told the story.

And Nurlan was most comfortable watching. Watching was a shield. If you stayed on the sidelines, you stayed safe.

That was what years of staffing parliamentarians had taught him. If you were in the audience, you weren't a part of the play. If you weren't part of the play, you couldn't die at the end. He had staffed parliamentarians from nearly every party. They came and went. He stayed.

His terminal vibrated.

I HAVE BEEN WATCHING THE NEWS. YOU ARE INSIDE THE BUILDING. TELL ME YOU ARE SAFE

"How did they solve their disagreements?" George asked Asel.

"They plowed their fields under. They poisoned their wells. They burned their houses down. Then they walked into the wilderness with their animals and became nomads. And as long as life was hard, they stayed happy. As long as they were always cold enough, always hungry enough. They never agreed on anything again after that vote in the village assembly house. But they were also never completely miserable. Until the Federation conquered us and forced us to live together in the cities again."

"Is that a folktale?" George asked.

And George only felt safe if he was asking questions.

Nurlan typed into his terminal:

FOR NOW

"It's just a story my father told. He used to say, 'We aren't happy unless we hear the wolves circling.' After independence, and back when Prime Ministers were still real people, he was Prime Minister twice. They even let him hold office for a year, once, before they no-confidenced him out. The day they held the vote, he walked up to the podium, howled like a wolf, and walked away. The cancer was eating away at him. He wanted peace, if only for a month or two. He'd fought his whole life for this place."

"Knowing it would never work?"

"Hoping it would. On his deathbed he told me, 'Help rebuild the village. It's time we nomads got some rest.'"

"You voted for rationalization," George said.

"I wanted to help end this. We did nothing but move from one gridlocked government to another. We couldn't do anything. We needed something drastic."

"And look where it got us," Jyldyz Kadyrova said. She had come over, had stood listening to the conversation for several minutes now. She jabbed a finger at George. "You technocrats in your gray suits promised us rationalization. You promised us we could be like you. You *built* this PM for us."

"Yes," George said. "We built it for you. The latest model. Superior, even, to anything we have where I come from."

"And now look where we are," Jyldyz said. "Is this rational? Is that what you would call it?"

From outside came the rattle of gunfire.

Atabek stood in front of the big screen. "There," he said, pointing at something. "There they are. Let's go, boys."

"What have you done?" Erlis Jeenbaev was on his feet now as well.

So was Nurlan, looking at the screen. On the square, men were running. Lying on the ground were several men who had stopped running forever.

"I've done what the rest of you were afraid to do. I've called in my boys to mop this up so we can all go home."

George winced as a boom sounded, muffled through the heavy curtains.

"More blood on the square," Erlis said. "And for what?"

"So we can get out of this building alive," said Atabek. "Don't you see? The PM is doing this on purpose. Someone has sabotaged its mind. We have to stop it."

On the screen there was a smear of fire as a Molotov cocktail splashed onto the pavement. The smear spread to a man. A man on fire. There was no one to help him: the others ran away as he tumbled on the ground, his heat burning a white hole in the screen's pixels. For a moment Nurlan imagined the burning man would drop through that hole, right into the room with them.

Energy bills. People were dying over energy bills.

"What you are suggesting isn't possible," George said. "Nobody can sabotage the mind of your PM. Once the mind is established, the data that comes in is sandboxed, scanned, sanitized. We monitor constantly for malicious code, attempts to interfere with its operations. An intrusion would be flagged immediately. You have the absolute-latest-model PM, and its systems are impenetrable . . ."

"So what *is* going on?" someone asked from the crowd.

Outside, the gunfire continued—but although it was not more than a few hundred meters from where they sat, it was still unreal. Still on a screen. Not here. Not in their world.

"I think the PM is doing what it was designed to do," George said.

"Cause a revolution?"

"No. We designed it to calculate human needs, and deconflict those needs in order to promote human thriving. Deconfliction of needs is the core of its assignment. But from the outside, it can look chaotic. When Greece rationalized, there were riots. People even died. But their PM pulled Greece out of debt, and did it without gutting their social services. Their PM saw ways forward no human mind could see. Their economy is humming along now. It's a success story. But they hung by their fingernails for a while. They almost voted to pull the plug. Rationalization won in a secret session by a single vote. It was our biggest test. And rationalization pulled through."

He straightened his spine, recrossed his legs, continued. Nurlan could tell he had said this before—reassured other parliaments in crisis. "Nobody—even the people who designed the Greek PM—could understand its actions. They thought it was sabotage too. People keep thinking of the Prime Ministers as having human attributes. We humans think everything that thinks should think *like us*. But it's a misrecognition. The Greek PM's decisions didn't follow human logic—and that is exactly why it got results."

"The Greek PM let people get killed over its decisions," said Jyldyz. "Which is the same as killing them itself."

"It acted without fear and without self-interest. It balanced the budget, protected labor rights, rid the system of corruption. Its decisions often appeared to be random or disordered. But that was because we couldn't follow the PM's process. The PM found a way. And your PM will find a way here too. You need to have faith."

"Faith?" someone said.

"Okay, 'faith' is the wrong word. Patience," George said. "Look, all over the world the PMs are making improvements. They are turning back the clock on climate change. They are sequestering carbon—something none of the previous governments could agree to—on a global scale. There is less carbon in the atmosphere than at any time since the nineteenth century. The PMs are breaking up human trafficking rings, improving infrastructure..." He paused, struggling for words. "It's like the story your father told, Asel. Humans poison our own wells. The irony that haunts our entire history is that *we humans* have been the ones standing in the way of our own happiness this whole time. Rationalization overcomes *us. It overcomes our faults.* All fighting does is make the process more painful. And this—"

"Greece may have been a mess," Atabek said, "but it was a *European* mess. This republic doesn't have the same history..."

IT IS LIVE ON THE NEWS, MY LOVE. IT IS GETTING WORSE

On the screen the burning man was now nothing more than a black, human-shaped outline.

"Your PM was made for you especially. Every PM is custom-designed to—"

Then there was a surge. A dark wave across the fallen figure. A roar.

YES. IT IS GETTING WORSE, Nurlan typed.

"What's happening?" Atabek asked.

"They are fighting back," Erlis Jeenbaev answered. He

pointed at another camera angle. "And your mercenaries are running away. I guess you didn't pay them enough."

"Those 'mercenaries' were all that was left between us and that mob," Atabek said. "Without them, those men will be through the security fences in a few hours. If not sooner."

"Violence wasn't going to do anything but bring more violence."

"You always root for the wrong side, Minister," said Atabek. "Maybe now you'll get what's coming to you."

I NEED TO HELP YOU

Nurlan typed:

I AM GOING TO BE ALL RIGHT

Jyldyz Kadyrova's terminal pinged, a message scrolling across its screen in red.

"The Prime Minister has doubled energy prices again."

"Well," said Jeenbaev. "It looks like we're *all* about to get what's coming to us."

10

LILIA
The Federation

Birds circled over the trees in agitation. Branches groaned beyond the edge of the clearing.

The thing emerged from the forest with a shudder of larch needles. It was three times as tall as any man. Broken twigs and needles of cedar and larch clung to its camouflage paint. Wet leaves and muck clung to its legs and its massive, birdlike feet.

The vestigial turret of its head turned toward her.

A forest walker.

They had been used during the Finnish border war, in the dense forest and bogs of the Karelian Isthmus. Images of that war were forbidden here, but she had seen one in a London gallery. The walker in winter camouflage, down on one knee, burned and coated in a thick layer of ice. Its operator on the ground nearby, staring up into the sky, one blue and frozen hand raised, shellacked with frost. The image of defeat.

The walker lumbered toward the Niva. Lilia had a clear

vision of her death—of the avian foot coming down on the car again and again.

It bent down on one knee. A curved door in its chest slid aside to reveal a padded compartment, a belted chair, and an old tank helmet leaking cotton batting from a rip in its side.

Mosquitoes crawled across the Niva's window glass.

She had nowhere else to go. Lilia opened the door of the car and clambered into the chest cavity of the walker.

The door of the walker's compartment slid shut too late to keep dozens of mosquitoes from coming in with her. As she belted herself into the seat she swatted and slapped.

By the time she had killed all the mosquitoes, the walker had left the clearing. Out a smeared porthole was a world of shifting tree trunks and gray-green shadow.

The forest walker's control panel had been torn out, leaving only the soldered stumps of the attachment points. Someone had taped a metal bottle to the bulkhead. Lilia drank, spilling as the walker lurched and tilted over the uneven ground and under branches. She strapped the helmet on.

What would her father imagine had happened to her? How would he survive without her?

He would have to limp, now, out of the house and down to the nearest store. Their apartment was on the fifth floor, with no elevator. By the time he reached the building's entrance he would be sweating, in pain. He would have to sit on the bench by the entrance to their stairwell, waiting for the pain to subside before continuing. That was what he'd done for years while Lilia was in London studying.

Her return had been a brief respite. Her disappearance would bring back the pain.

He would be terrified for her, but there was nothing he could do. No inquiries to be made, no one to turn to. He would report her as missing, because not to do so would make it worse for him, and for her if she was caught.

The end had begun for him: Without her, he would have to rely on neighbors to buy food. It would register with the system as a lack of self-sufficiency. His social credit score would begin to drop, limiting what he could buy in the stores or even eat when bought by others, pinging the terminals of people who passed him with warnings not to engage with him. Once his social credit score dropped below a certain point, he would be entered into the lottery. When his number came up, it was off to one of the PPECs, where they'd have him assembling drone circuit boards sixteen hours a day, sleeping on three inches of recycled plastifoam mattress spread over a concrete bunk.

Or on the floor, with no mattress at all, in one of the worst camps.

Once that happened, he'd be dead within a month.

She had killed him. When she left the apartment she had saved herself and killed him.

Again, Lilia imagined the circles paced by social offenders on "conditional release." Even those circles weren't the real story: The loops people were contained in were smaller than that. They were contained in their own skulls. It wasn't a *percentage* of the population that was imprisoned—it was *everyone.*

Everyone, from the people with glowing social credit scores that allowed them access to shops selling buttery smoked salmon and imported luxuries to the people no longer able to leave their houses, forced to subsist on the charity of neighbors or overpriced state drone deliveries of cheap flour and tea that tasted like sawdust. They all knew the rules. You don't criticize. You don't differ. You go to work, you come home, you read the right books, you repeat the right lies to your children. You go to church. You say the right prayers. You celebrate the right holidays with the right people.

Everyone was a prisoner. Some in the PPECs, some on "conditional release," all of them prisoners in their own heads. It wasn't freedom or limitation people chose. It was degrees of punishment.

Rain thudded against the walker's hull. They were wading through a bog. She looked out through the blurred porthole into a liquid world. The sky hammered down, agitating the stagnant pools to a cold boil. The walker picked its muddy way across, sometimes up to its porthole in water as it wound through the trunks of drowned trees.

No roads here, no paths in or out: this was the true taiga. It had always been there, looming past the shoulders of the roads, rolling under the wings of her plane. But now she was inside it.

Swallowed by it. In the belly of this thing, and in the belly of the taiga. In the forest that had never been real to her. The endless, immortal forest of fairy tales. Of huts on chicken legs, fences made of human skulls, bears that were human and then bears again, crows that told riddles, things transformed and transforming.

She drifted off, exhausted, lulled by the drumming of the rain, the rocking and sloshing of the walker's movement through the bog.

Then the walker jerked unexpectedly. She was awake again, thinking of Palmer.

Even before the flour, the Birnam device, all of this, she had tried not to think of him. He was a part of London. A part of what was lost to her. He was gone the way her professors, slouched in their English offices lined with real books, were gone. Gone the way the gleaming laboratories with their machines more powerful than anything she'd ever been given access to here were gone.

When she took the dioramas home to Palmer and showed them to him, he'd had no idea what he might be looking at. To him, they were nothing more than a VR toy. He'd had no idea she had done what no one had ever managed to do before.

And how could he know? What could he know of the things she worked on? What could he understand of them?

She sometimes thought she had chosen to be with Palmer precisely because he would understand nothing of what she worked on. He was suited so perfectly to her precisely because he offered her privacy. With him, she could be a regular person, like everyone else—and also continue to be who she really was, without being questioned.

He allowed her ease and room to think. He did not pry and poke at her, force her to explain things still half-formed in her own mind.

But what that also meant was that Palmer was unprepared for any of this. How would he have handled her disappearance, about which he could do nothing? Did he think she had run away from him? He couldn't think that. Did he understand she had been taken?

She had left the dioramas with him. And they *worked*.
The white rose.

All right—she had left them. But wasn't that the best place for them? They would stay hidden, because he would never understand what they were. And she could not have taken them with her.

She imagined them on the table, like a couple of knickknacks. What did they register now? What did her screen show him?

And what would Palmer do with them once he decided she was never coming back?

The white rose on the table. Perfect and colorless as a hole in the world.

I don't know why I bought it for you, really. I was just passing by the florist and saw it in the window.

She had a vision of the dioramas sitting among the clutter of candlesticks, toy cars, and dusty radios in the window of some London junk shop.

Maybe that would be the best place for the dioramas. Hidden in plain sight until their displays went dark forever.

No one would ever know what they had been. That the mood displays were nothing but sleight of hand, fables, a mask for what was underneath.

No one would ever know what she had managed to do. The puzzle she had solved that no one else could.

"Where are you taking me?" she said aloud. "Who do you belong to?"

As if in response, the walker lurched. Her head smacked against the side of the compartment. The padding of the tank helmet dulled the impact, but it still hurt.

She braced herself against the side of the compartment and peered through the porthole. The walker tilted, clambering over a deadfall.

Beyond, under the canopy of trees—a house. An izba.

It took a moment for Lilia to register what was strange about the place.

It was perfect. That was it. From the immaculate, brightly painted fretwork around the windows and the eaves down to the sawn pickets of the fence enclosing it. Perfect, as no izba that had seen even one season in the taiga could possibly be.

The walker halted. Lilia unstrapped and climbed down, still feeling the world rock unsteadily.

Glossy. That was what was most strange about the little house. It shone in the light through the trees. Not like wood.

It wasn't wood at all. The building had been printed. It was made of plasticrete. The ridges showed where each layer had been laid down.

But there were even embroidered curtains in the windows. And smoke rose from its chimney.

The door opened.

11

NURLAN
The Republic

Something enormous moved across the square, cutting a path through the crowds. People scattered out of its way. At first it looked like a bear, an enormous bear, on its hind legs.

The thing *moved* like a bear, lumbering forward. Then it sped up, black and fast, long arms knuckled down to the pavement.

The way it moved changed. It now charged the way a silverback gorilla would—but not quite the way a silverback gorilla would. It glitched and shifted. He could glimpse, in its movements, the replicated movement of other animals, along with innovations of its own.

An assault walker. Where could they have gotten one of them? The black paint told Nurlan it was police.

Someone said, "Tell me that thing is one of ours."

The protesters—the rioters, the revolutionaries—fled from

its path. The thing accelerated, slamming into the reinforced fence surrounding the building.

"No," someone said. "It's theirs."

So the police were on the other side now. Some of the police, at least. Or this thing had been stolen from them.

In the last revolution, before rationalization, the police had put down a riot with two walkers. The things had left a hundred rioters dead on the square.

Not "rioters." People. People on the wrong side.

And those things hadn't killed protesters—the people piloting them had. Either a person inside, or a person at a distance, piloting them like a drone, or a person who had set their parameters, wound the monsters up, and sent them into the world.

Any way you looked at it, a human being was doing the killing. The machine was nothing but a tool.

The assault walker yanked at the fence. The reinforced steel buckled. Now its movements had no metaphor. No animal moved the way it moved, and no human.

For the first time that day, Nurlan felt real fear. Visceral fear that caused his muscles to seize and narrowed his vision. That thing would be *inside* the building soon. It would be where he was.

You can save them. And save yourself. I know how you can shut the PM down

He had to type the message three times before he got it right.

How can you know that?

I told you what I do

Yes, she'd told him. Secret work. Government security systems. She'd let him see the edges of it.

She might know. It could be true. If it was, it might be the only way.

The walker backed up. Masonry lay in the square. The fence had buckled. The walker had pulled the posts from their concrete moorings, but the fence was not yet breached.

Not yet, but it would be. How long did they have? A minute? Five minutes?

YOU NEED TO TRUST ME

I DO

CAN YOU LEAVE WITHOUT THEM SEEING YOU?

Everyone watched the walker onscreen, battering down the last barrier between them and the crowd. Death, smashing its way closer to them. Arms wrapped around themselves as if that might save them. Hands covering their eyes as if it might help. But *doing* nothing.

Stiff as a group of statues, they watched death coming for them.

Nurlan stood up.

They didn't see him.

They had never seen him.

He walked to the side door, then out into a corridor stained red with emergency lighting. Papers were scattered on the floor.

He imagined he could feel the building vibrate as the walker threw itself against the fence again. Not possible. But even here, he could hear the sound of the crowd outside.

His hands shook, but he was calm.

This was what it was like, then, to act. To stand up and do something.

I AM OUT

WHAT CORRIDOR ARE YOU IN?

8B

Go to the end of the hall. Don't go to the main stairwell door. There is another door. Painted gray. Locked. There will be a keypad

Nurlan passed abandoned offices, their doors hanging open, heavy furniture heaped in the dark.

There it was—the door and the pad. Not with numbers—with letters.

The sequence is TEHDRAATM

He punched it in.

Metal stairs coiled down into the dark, half-lit by diode strips spiraling down with it.

Hurry. They have breached the fence. And they are bringing fire

A scream came from the hall where the parliamentarians were gathered. Whose? He could not tell.

He closed the door behind him. It was silent except for ticking, like the sound of metal expanding and contracting.

Like the sound of metal's pulse.

Quickly

For a moment, his legs would not move. He would not be able to do it. Then the steps clanked under his feet, loud in the semi-dark.

He had the feeling of winding down into the gullet of some animal. The metal walls clicked and popped, expanding and contracting under a hidden pressure.

Could it know he was here? Could it sense his presence?

What happens when I shut it down?

He could stop. He could go back up. Wait with the others for what was coming.

WHAT WILL HAPPEN IF YOU DON'T SHUT IT DOWN? YOU SAW THAT THING ON THE SQUARE. YOU KNOW WHAT IT CAN DO

Death, crushed in the clamping claw or under the stomping foot of the walker. Death by smoke and fire.

There was a sound in the stairwell. A despairing squawk. Nurlan realized he was making it.

He typed:

WHY DOES IT HAVE TO BE ME?

BECAUSE YOU ARE THE ONLY ONE BRAVE ENOUGH

There was something no one had ever accused him of being.

THE OTHERS WILL KEEP ARGUING UNTIL THE SMOKE FILLS THEIR LUNGS AND THEY DIE NURLAN

I can't.

He had almost typed the words. He was surprised not to see them on his screen.

YOU CAN

It was always like this. She could anticipate his thoughts, and he could anticipate hers.

In a month, they would be together. He would see her for the first time. See the sliding doors at the airport open.

It was not fear of his own death that pushed him forward, but the fear that he would not be standing there when Hazal came through those doors.

Then he was at the bottom of the stairs. What had he been expecting to find here? A door, an entrance?

There was no door. There was nothing here but a rectangle of polished metal on the wall.

DO YOU SEE IT?

THERE IS NOTHING HERE

THE ACCESS POINT ON THE WALL. PRESS YOUR TERMINAL AGAINST IT

He placed his terminal against the wall. His screen came alive, blinding in the dark as windows opened and closed. It went black. It stayed dark for what must have been a minute before a keypad appeared on it.

THE SEQUENCE IS FIFTY NUMBERS LONG. I WILL TYPE IT OUT TO YOU IN CHUNKS. IF YOU MAKE A MISTAKE WE WILL NEED TO START OVER

I WON'T MAKE A MISTAKE

And he did not. When he was done, the keypad disappeared. That was all. Nurlan looked at the blank rectangle on the wall. He looked up at the coil of diodes spiraling up into the dark.

SHOULDN'T SOMETHING HAPPEN?

IT ALREADY HAS. YOU HAVE BROUGHT DOWN THE RATIONALIST GOVERNMENT. THE PM IS GONE. NOW LET'S GET YOU OUT OF HERE

WE HAVE TO LET THE OTHERS KNOW

IT IS TOO LATE FOR THEM

WHAT DO YOU MEAN?

THE BUILDING IS ALREADY ON FIRE. THAT THING IS ALREADY INSIDE. BUT I KNOW A WAY OUT

HOW CAN YOU KNOW THESE THINGS?

IT IS MY JOB TO KNOW. I AM SENDING YOU A SCHEMATIC. YOU DON'T HAVE LONG. WE WILL MEET, AND I WILL TELL YOU EVERYTHING. BUT FOR THAT TO HAPPEN, YOU MUST SURVIVE

12

ELMIRA
The Union

"And where are the dioramas now?" Elmira asked.

The professor's desk was near the window, with a view down into a dismal concrete quadrangle, crossed by students hurrying to get elsewhere. "She must have taken them with her. I wouldn't know. Maybe she wanted to test the distance—see if it really was unlimited."

"You said they were a technology you had never seen before. You said: 'The problem with trying to evaluate her work was that not one of us could understand it. We weren't even smart enough for her to explain it to us.'"

"But this isn't some *classified facility*. She was a student on exchange, attending university in a free country. She could do what she wanted. And I didn't expect . . ."

"What?"

"I didn't expect her to *succeed* at it. And I didn't expect her to disappear."

"So she succeeded."

"I think she did."

"And she didn't tell you where she was going?"

"She told me she was going home, to pay a last visit to her father. We all believed she was coming back."

"That seems naïve, given where she is from and what she may have invented."

She watched his face. His expression told her that this was the first time he had considered it—the first time it had occurred to him that what Lilia had done might be dangerous to her, that the Federation might, in fact, be more than just some distant producer of bad news. That it might step right into real life and make someone disappear.

"Yes," the professor said, scraping his thumb along the cable of his sweater. "It does seem naïve. I mean, it does *now*. But things always seem obvious after they happen. We witnessed an extraordinary moment here. Lilia found a way to look into a system from a distance and know its structure *in the moment*. She did what no one else could do. And she demonstrated the persistence of the connection. When she disappeared, she had already been running the experiment for months."

"The experiment—you mean pictures in boxes of people rowing boats. Little metaphorical scenes of a mental pattern. It doesn't seem like anything more than a game."

"You misunderstand."

"Do I?"

"The scenes are a screen projected onto the surface. They aren't the information: they conceal it. She called the pictures 'the scrim'—like the semitransparent screen in a theater set. The scenes project an image. A metaphor, as you said, for a generalized state. But underneath the scrim is the real pattern, the *full* pattern, which can only be seen when the dioramas are linked up to the full system Lilia invented. Then they allow us to look into a person's *skull*. To read the state of their entire connectome. To watch their thoughts *as they happen, at the synaptic level*."

"And who else knows?"

"I was her mentor. I don't think anyone does. Unless she told the boyfriend."

"Do you think she did?"

"I doubt it. I mean—she may have told him *some* of it, but not the whole thing. I doubt he would have understood."

"What makes you say that?"

"We had dinner once. He was . . . well, I'll call him *average*. Let's leave it at that."

"And could she already have found a way to do more than *look* at people's thoughts? Could she have found a way to *change* them?"

"No," the professor said. "Not this soon. It would take years."

But the tone of his voice told her he wasn't certain.

"How many years?"

"I don't know. Five? Ten? New technologies don't have a set time. Maybe never."

He didn't want to believe she had done it. So he didn't.

The professor was looking out the window again. People crossed and recrossed the gray quadrangle, headed elsewhere.

"Spooky action at a distance," he said.

"What's that?"

"It's what Einstein called entanglement. He didn't believe

in it. And I feel like even though we've proven it exists over and over again, we don't believe in it either. Not really." The professor gestured out the window at the students passing and repassing through the non-place his office looked down into. "I don't think if we believed in what is going on at the quantum level we could go on the way we do. I think we only believe in the quantum world while we are running an experiment or writing a paper. Then it fades away. We have breakfast in our macro world. We get dressed and do other things quantum realities make meaningless. Every time we look away from that quantum world, we disavow it. We couldn't live otherwise."

"Don't lose faith, Professor," Elmira said.

"What do you mean?"

"Don't lose faith in our *macro world*. It's the only world we've got."

Out in the quadrangle one of the students stopped, looking at a terminal. Then another. Then another. Two of the students were talking. One held their terminal up to the other. They watched what was happening there together.

"Yes, I can talk now," Elmira said.

The voice was the smallest whisper in the air.

"No, that conversation has ended . . . moments ago . . . Yes, I can talk here."

The students stood in the quadrangle below, watching their screens.

"There was nothing left on the machines in the laboratory at the university. Our crawlers have been through there. She had it set up so that if she did not access the data for a certain period, it destroyed itself."

Pause.

"To her, I think it would have been a routine precaution."

Pause.

"I can move there in advance, then. To intercept. Certainly, he isn't here any longer. He's left London. If we have even an educated guess as to where he is headed, I should try to get ahead of him."

The wasp landed on the window. It walked across the glass, obscuring one student and then another, as if comparing its size to them. She plucked it from the pane with the pair of tongs and placed it in its cylinder.

"Yes, I am still at the university. In his office. Yes, that's done."

Anyone who looked at the professor would think he had fallen asleep at his desk. The light through the window was as gray as the concrete quadrangle below. Dismal light on a dead man.

"I'll catch the next flight," Elmira said.

The voice was the intermittent buzz of a fault in the wiring, behind the walls.

"I think it happened while we were still talking. I saw people . . . outside, reacting to the news. I agree: it's unexpected. But nothing is infallible. There must have been a miscalculation. They should never have tried to spread the PMs outside their own system."

At the center of the quadrangle was a sapling.

Its leaves were turning yellow.

She had not noticed it before, this tree that felt what she could not feel. This sapling in its shade that understood autumn had arrived. It had gotten that information before she had. Before anyone had. It had known it. Where? In its roots?

On the surface of its bark? What did it mean for a tree to *know* a thing?

From her high angle she could see the screens of the terminals the students were gathering around. She could see fire on the screens: a building burning, the image of it cast out into the world.

The students gathered around the screens as if the fire were giving off real warmth.

A campfire. A bonfire. A hearth.

BOOK TWO
THE CHILDREN OF SAREZ

When a brown hare senses a fox stalking it, it does not run. It stands tall and faces its pursuer. The slower fox then knows it now has no chance of catching the faster hare and breaks off the pursuit. This saves both of them the danger of a pointless chase.

In the animal world, cooperation can even exist between predator and prey.

Here in our human world, the predator will pursue its prey until both are destroyed in fury.

—ZOYA ALEKSEYEVNA VELIKANOVA, *The Forever Argument*

13

ZOYA
The Federation

"I'm following you off into the forest," Zoya said, "and I realize that I don't even know your name."

They had walked for a quarter of an hour. They both had mosquito nets over their faces, but the woman, her Birnam device still activated, was also still half-ghost to Zoya, the birch-bark skeleton of the trees visible through her.

Let the lovely Swan Maiden stand before me! Let her body be seen through her feathers, let her bones be seen through her body, let it be seen through her bones how the marrow flows from bone to bone.

A line from a fairy tale. As if Zoya's grandmother Alla, long dead, were here in the taiga reading it to her.

Through a cloud of hungry mosquitoes, the woman said, "Call me Ella."

"Where are you taking me, Ella?"

But even as she said the words, she saw the destination.

There, in a clearing, was an izba. Impossible that it should have been there, but there it was, in every sawn-wood detail, its eaves bright as flowers.

Inside, Zoya was led to a chair like the chair in a dentist's office. Around it was a tangle of machines and wires, of blinking diodes and metal racks of more machines.

Ella hung their mosquito hats up on pegs near the door. The izba was not made of wood: it was printed. The "whitewash" on the walls glistened, the not-quite-even strata of its printing visible.

"Are you comfortable?" Ella asked. "Can I get you something to eat? To drink?"

"How long has this been here?"

"A few days. When we are finished, drones will spray an agent on the izba that will dissolve its chemical bonds. Within hours no trace will be left."

"And where will you go?"

Ella set a thing upon Zoya's head. An object like a wreath or a crown, if such a thing were made of twisted wire and sensors.

"I will continue my work. I am a part of a larger network, Zoya Alekseyevna. I'm nothing more than a worker bee."

"Not part of a network, then—part of a swarm."

"Aren't we all?"

"And what will you do with me—or with this copy of me?"

Ella was bent over her, adjusting the wire crown. A terminal came alive. On its screen was a web or a map—but denser than that, more irregular. A tangle of tangles. Zoya was looking into her own mind.

"We'll make a country we can all be proud of. At last."

"Ambitious."

"Yes. Finally, we may be ambitious enough to change things."

"And if I refuse?"

Ella straightened and looked Zoya in the eyes. Through her the machine diodes blinked, as if embedded in her flesh. "You won't. Because you know who we are. We are the people who *act*. The ones you wrote about. The ones your writing calls out to. The agents of change."

The ones she was calling out to.

Zoya's own work had always been stale to her, empty. She had always thought it would have been better if someone else were burdened with these ideas. Someone more qualified to put them into words. But sometimes, maybe, she wrote something worthwhile.

We cannot wait. We must act immediately, and take the consequences. We must debate their results, and act again. Action cannot be the product of a final conclusion. Action and argument must be bound up together, driving one another forward, each correcting the other's course.

Action and argument together form an experiment, and nothing but constant experimentation will get us where we need to be. The system that contains us is not threatened by what we think of it. It is threatened by what we do about it. And the time for doing is always now.

She had believed that writing itself was an action. But she had stopped believing that: She had come to see her writing as nothing but empty words. A delaying tactic. Something to do to hide her own impotence in the face of unchanging, unconquerable, indifferent state power.

In the early days, she had gone out into the streets to be beaten for her beliefs, like a pilgrim taking communion. But soon enough, they had asked her not to go with them anymore. She had become too big a prize for the regime to take in an arrest, too vital to the cause to be lost to a penal colony or killed in some scuffle, some meaningless battle in the longer war.

And she had accepted their offer. She had stayed behind and written. She had stopped acting.

"Will it hurt?"

"No. You might feel strange, but it won't be painful."

"I am ready to start, then." She grasped the arms of the chair. Ella had said there would be no pain, but Zoya knew there was always pain.

"We have already started. You may experience memories. Some of them may seem very real and present to you. That's a side effect."

The floor of the izba had changed—where there had been wood planks, there were now cobblestones.

Cobblestones, and blood on the cobblestones. She knew whose blood it was. She knew that, when she looked up, the red walls would be there. The red walls, and the walls of riot shields in front of those walls, and in front of that wall of shields the fallen protesters. And among them Yuri, who was dead.

But she saw none of that. She could hear it all—at a distance, as if it were somewhere outside the izba. As if the protest were occurring here, in the taiga, somewhere out there in the trees.

She could *feel* that moment. The feeling was bodily—the terror, the wide-eyed terror, worse than physical pain.

Then the flood of endorphins into her system: The feeling of being young. Of being young and in action. The cold air on her cheeks.

The fear, yes. The horror of Yuri falling to the stones, yes—but also that feeling of *action*. Of *possibility*—because even if Yuri was dead, *she* was alive, and as the crowd surged around her, pushed back by the row of riot shields, and then pushing *them* back—it felt as if they *could* break the line. As if even the red-brick walls could be broken through. As if those bricks were paper to be torn. As if the crowd, the mass of them all together, was that strong.

In a moment, the crowd would break. The rout would begin. Yuri would not be the last person killed that day as they fled and were beaten, rounded up, pushed against walls, battered to death in police vans.

But none of those moments were *this* moment. Of power and action. Of strength and possibility. Of rage and potential.

In the years that followed, they would come to understand the truth—that the days when protests worked, and authoritarian regimes dissolved before the determined voices of freedom or melted away against the inundations of resistance, were gone.

Once the regimes had been emptied of ideology—once power became about power alone—there was no breaking them. They had no morality. They did not become disgusted with themselves and turn away from killing. Their will did not break, no matter how many protesters they had to arrest, beat, or kill. They had no conscience, and so they were not stung by guilt.

The only thing they feared was the loss of their own power.

They understood the simple rule, proven time and again: to hold on to power, never give up power.

The regimes had learned, from watching how other autocratic systems were toppled, that compromise was death. They made no reforms. They promised nothing. They simply jailed, beat, harassed, and killed as many people as was necessary.

In the years that followed, Zoya and her allies would come to understand that they would never win. Their resistance to power was purely symbolic. It demonstrated to others that the human will could not be broken. It gave hope to those not yet locked into authoritarian systems. But here, in this country, the time in which change was possible was long past. There was only the President, forever. And though his face might change, they all knew he was the same man behind every new mask.

They ran out of allies. They ran out of recruits to their cause. The population wanted nothing more to do with resistance: they bent their necks forever. They closed the doors to their little worlds and tried to survive.

For a few years, there were still the kitchen conversations. Zoya and those of them who were left sat around late-night tables and discussed what they called options, unable to admit to themselves that those options no longer existed.

With each new war the Federation waged on a neighbor, they fantasized about a defeat. About foreign intervention, regime change. They pondered violence none of them were capable of.

With each change in the President's health, they yearned for a palace coup. That, they decided, was the only thing that could rid the country of him. Someone on the inside. Someone near enough to him to slip the knife in.

But even back then, dead Yuri whispered in her ear:

"You'll exchange one tsar for another, that's all."

"Nothing can last forever" was her response to his ghost.

"Nothing has to. He's as interchangeable as a rotten plank in a ship. They all are."

"Then we burn the ship."

Yuri lay on the cobblestones with a mouth full of blood. "The ship can be replaced as well."

The cobblestones were gone. A voice said, "Please don't move."

When she looked up to see where the voice had come from, Yuri was across the table from her. The voice had not been his.

He lifted his coffee cup to his lips and blew across the surface of the cup. Such detail: She could see the waveforms his breath created across the surface of the coffee. His swollen eye, beginning to close.

They were in their kitchen. It was a winter evening when he still lived. The snow blew through the light of the streetlamps outside. A man was walking a dog. The man had his collar up. She thought, again, as she had in that moment—*the man can turn his collar up, but the dog goes naked.*

Another political idea. By this time in her life, everything was political. She processed everything into material for her pamphlets, her manifestos, the thing that was becoming her book.

Next to Yuri's saucer was a bag of frozen peas he was using as an ice pack.

"Don't worry," Yuri said. "I will be all right."

"Will you?"

Before that winter was over, Yuri would be dead.

They killed him, and then did not even allow people to bring flowers to where he had fallen. When people found that was forbidden, they brought flowers to a crumbling monument to a tank brigade, housed in an anonymous square on the edge of the city. The monument was of a single man, a grenade in each hand, standing before an oncoming tank. They put their flowers there, piles of them that the police threw into trucks and hauled away to the city dump.

Even that small act of disobedience was unforgivable. The police scanned the faces of everyone who had placed flowers there and at other monuments around the country. The Investigative Committee knocked on doors for months afterward, arresting thousands of people. Some never came home.

No act of resistance was too small to escape punishment. And they never even allowed her to see his body. They burned him, and she was sure his ashes went where the flowers went—or worse.

Yuri was gone again. Ella stood over her, lifting the crown from Zoya's head and placing it aside.

"Are we done?" Zoya asked.

Can I go back? she wanted to ask. *Just for a moment? To be with him a little longer?*

"Yes. We are finished."

The traces were still there—chemical traces of the rage she had felt on the square, the love and grief of seeing Yuri again.

"You were right about the memories. It was like—being there again."

Ella withdrew a subterminal from the larger array and placed it into a waterproof bag.

"Is that all of me?" Zoya asked. "Does all of me fit in there?"

"With room to spare."

"Strange that in the end we are so small. I remembered Yuri, my husband. Fragments of him: the moment he was killed, and then a memory from before. I have always wondered if there was a time when I could have prevented his death. The idea haunts me. But I also know that if I had, they would have arrested and tortured him sooner or later. And he would have betrayed me. The others all betrayed me in the end. They had to. His death saved me from that sorrow, at least. And in a way, it saved him."

"Yes," Ella said. "You wrote that in your book—that it is better to die in action. Because no one resists, in the end. Once the state gets hold of us, they take everything. *'We will betray our friends, and more—we will give up people who were never even there. We will do anything to make the torture stop. We think we won't, but we will. We will do anything to put a stop to the pain.'* Do you still believe that?"

"I do," Zoya said.

Ella put a hand on her shoulder. "Good."

The drones came an hour later. A swarm of them, the buzz of their rotors barely audible over the buzz of the billions of summer mosquitoes among the trees in the dusk. The drones' spray nozzles swept over the izba. The roof began to melt. The eaves drooped like spun sugar held over a flame. The structure warped. The walls deformed, sagging to the ground.

The swarm circled. Their nozzles swiveled, aiming their disintegrating spray over the terminals, the racks of equipment, the dead woman in the chair.

Her face drained away. Her skull grinned into the coins of sunlight falling through the trees. Her form wilted, her flesh streamed, her bones ran liquid and flowed with the rest of the izba into the soil, into the roots and the fungal networks, until all that was left of her was a dwindling pool of color on the forest floor, into which leaves began to fall.

14

LILIA
The Federation

Lilia recognized the war-burned and reconstructed face of the man who stood in the door of the izba. His mask of laboratory-grown skin, pink and unlined. His aged, inflamed eyes.

"I knew you would come back," he said. "You are not the kind to stay in the West, where nothing matters."

She stood halfway between the walker and the izba's open door. Her feet would not move.

"Things matter there," she said, as if taking up the argument started years ago.

The mask made a show of teeth that might have been a smile.

"Not for you. If they did, you wouldn't have returned."

She still could not move. Mosquitoes surged against her face and whined in her ears.

"You are afraid," the man continued. "But if killing you were our aim, we would not have bothered with the journey or the expense. We could as easily have placed a bomb in that bag of flour as a Birnam device. My name is Gleb. Now come inside, before the forest eats you alive."

Inside the izba, there was a slight gloss to everything. It was a 3D-printed simulacrum of a traditional house. But where the stove should be, the axe-split furniture, the embroidered curtains, there were terminals and equipment on racks, white countertops, swivel chairs.

The house contained a replica of her laboratory from the university in London. Every machine she had worked on there. And along with them, a copy of every machine she had *ever* worked on. There was the battered terminal from her local university, here in the Federation. Her first terminal, bought by her father with money scraped together for months, was reproduced here. There was even a terminal she had sometimes used at a friend's house after school.

There was a woman here, not much older than Lilia.

A mosquito that had found its way in buzzed its eternal question in Lilia's ear. On a printed table to one side of the room was a pot of tea and a plate of cookies.

Was the teapot printed as well? It was. As was the plate. At least the cookies were not.

Everything hurt. She now felt every jolt of the Niva, every jarring tilt of the walker. She felt like one big bruise.

"I am Taisiya. Sit," the woman said. "Drink a cup of tea. Drink, and eat. You need it."

Lilia slumped into the chair. Taisiya poured a cup of strong black tea. Lilia drank it. It was just cool enough that she could get it down her throat. She crammed the cookies into her mouth, one after another.

"Hunger is the best salt," Gleb said.

Hunger is the best salt . . .

Her father had said that to her. They were eating a late lunch. Some terrible little roadside café, on the way to a destination now forgotten. They ate stale sandwiches of bland sausage and butter. The trip had been held up by an accident on the road, and the sandwiches, combined with the thermos of tea that was their only other sustenance, tasted heavenly.

Her father.

Gleb and Taisiya watched her eat. She poured the second cup of tea herself.

"It doesn't have to be for nothing," Taisiya said.

"What doesn't?"

"The battering you've taken. The trip here. The imprisonment before that, the arrest, the loss of the life you built in London."

Lilia's father knew, by now, that she was gone for good.

No. It was worse than that. They had him by now. Or they would soon. She was gone, and the state would demand an explanation.

She had left him with nothing to tell them.

Maybe, she tried to tell herself, his ignorance would save him from the worst of it. Once they understood he wasn't lying, there was no need to do anything further to him. They would zero out his social credit score and toss him in a PPEC . . .

Where he would be dead soon enough. He would never survive life in there, with his hip the way it was.

Her father would be dead soon, because of her. He had raised her alone. To thank him, she'd gotten him killed.

"Can you help my father? He isn't a part of any of this. Can you get him out, the way you got me out?"

Gleb shook his head. "We cannot get him out. But perhaps we can help him in some way. I will find out."

"Anything. Please. Can you let him know that I'm alive? I don't want him to think the state has me. That I was disappeared, like so many others."

"I will find out."

The teacup made an artificial clack as she set it down on its saucer.

"Do what you can for my father, and I will help you. I will give you whatever you want. Name it, and I will give it to you."

But she knew what they wanted. The machines reproduced here had told her that. There was only one thing she had done in her life that no one else had done.

Had they even considered what would happen to her father? Had her father's life ever even figured into any of their equations?

"We will do what we can for your father," Gleb said. "I promise it. It may not be much, but we will try."

She remembered her father in church, a little more than a week ago, his face a mask of pain. When was the last time they had been able to speak meaningfully to one another? How long had it been since she had been able to tell him something real? Since they had shared a memory together?

Would they ever have that again?

An impossible world rose up in her mind for a moment,

in which the state crumbled and both of them were free. In which they sat down across a table without fear and simply talked. In which, incredibly, he met Palmer and *they* talked.

Then, as suddenly as it had arisen, this impossibility was wiped away.

"Then tell me what you want from me."

"The dioramas," Gleb said. "Let's start there. What can they do—in your own words?"

"No."

"What do you mean, 'no'?"

"I mean that's not where we are starting. You must *know* what the dioramas do. If you didn't know those things, I wouldn't be here. No. First, *you* are going to tell me who *you* are and what you want from me. You were there when I was given my exit visa. You've been watching me since before I left for London."

"Yes," the man said. "We have."

"I didn't get out of this country myself. You *let* me out."

"We helped, yes. We removed your name from certain databases. It was not easy. You are the child of a dissident."

Hearing her father referred to as a dissident sounded strange. All he had ever done was obey the rules. As long as she had known him, he had been cautious, obedient. When she had even mildly criticized something—a teacher at school, a lesson she despised, even something as simple as the starched stiffness of her school uniform's apron, he shook his head and repeated, over and over, the same phrase: *Such things are not for us to change.*

He never spoke about the punishment battalion, or what

had come before to get him there. Whatever it was that he had done. Had he been, once, something like this man? Like this woman?

Dissident.

She tried to imagine it, but the image wouldn't square with that of her *papa*—the quiet man who had worked odd jobs all her childhood so that the two of them could scrape by.

"Why did you help me?"

"We saw a chance you might be able to do something no one else has done. We glimpsed it in your experiments here, though they were crude models run on outdated machines. You were trying to see into a system from a distance. But it was a puzzle you weren't going to be able to solve in our country."

"How did you know I could solve it elsewhere?"

"We did not. We believed there was a *chance* you could solve it," Gleb said. "With the right equipment. With time, and freedom."

"The odds don't seem right. I wasn't that close before I left here. I believed I was onto it, but I was careful to mask it too. How could you have known?"

"We bet on many people," Taisiya said. "You were only one of them."

"How many people?"

"That's not for you to know."

Were there six or seven other Lilias out there? A dozen? Twenty? Living free lives in free countries, safe because they had failed to do what she had done?

"But how did you know I would come back?"

"We didn't," Taisiya said. "And your coming back has

complicated everything. Any reasonable person . . ." She let the sentence hang in the air.

"Most people," Gleb said, "would have stayed in London. Even if their father was ill. Most people would have understood there was nothing that could be done for him. We never imagined you would return."

"I knew there was nothing I could do for my father," said Lilia. "But I needed to see him again. That's all. I needed to say a proper goodbye."

"Of all the stupid, empty gestures," Taisiya said. "Of all the insane—"

The man put his hand up. "No," the man said. "I understand. Being with your father one last time. That's not nothing."

"It was worse than nothing. He was so angry with me for coming back. I have never seen him so angry. And he was right to be. Coming back here was the worst thing I could have done."

"Yes, it was. And here we all are," Taisiya said.

"Don't mind Taisiya. She is tired."

Gleb sat down across from Lilia. "You are right: you are owed an explanation. But you see, Taisiya is tired and angry. This conversation was supposed to happen in London. We were supposed to find you in a cozy little café there. We would start a casual chat. We would invite you to a place where we would not be watched.

"There, we would have a quiet, civilized conversation. We would ask you for the dioramas and for the code supporting their operations. We would tell you why—some of why, enough to convince you—and you would be happy to give them to us. Then you would go back to Palmer, to your snug little flat—"

"Your snug little *life*," Taisiya interrupted.

"To your laboratory at the university," Gleb continued. "You would continue your work—but not on the dioramas. We would ask you to stop working on those. Not forever, but for a time. For five years, say. Enough time to give us a head start. And we would compensate you. We would put a good deal of money in your bank account. Perhaps you and Palmer would travel. Things would happen here, but those things would not concern you. Your life would continue. Not only unchanged, but improved."

"I wrecked it all by coming back. Not only for myself, not only for my father . . . but even for you."

"An understatement," Taisiya said.

"I understand why you did what you did," Gleb said. "But in the Federation it is all"—he gestured around at the sheen of the printed house, its printed furniture. The gesture seemed to take in the forest outside as well, the mud-smeared walker standing sentinel beyond the door, the PPECs, the cities filled with slaves, the government itself—"so much more complicated."

Palmer. "What about Palmer? You could send someone. You could ask him for the dioramas. And you could tell him where I am. That I am safe."

"You think you are safe?" Taisiya stared at the ceiling with a look Lilia could read: *Who are these people?* "Palmer had the brilliant idea of running all over London looking for help getting you back. He brought enough attention to himself that the Federation's agents got onto him. And the dioramas.

We managed to extract him from London without his getting himself killed. He should have arrived at the waypoint by now, but I doubt he will last long. There's no way. Eventually he'll make a mistake, and they'll have him."

Her father. And now Palmer. She'd killed him as well. All because she had decided to come back.

"If you had stayed," Taisiya said. "If you had stayed put for a few more months . . ."

"You were there," Lilia said to Gleb. "When I was leaving here. You *told* me I would come back. As if you were putting a curse on me."

"I was playing a part," Gleb said. "It was an empty line. Nobody returns. Those who can get out, stay out. That's the only reason they let people leave in the first place. It is the easiest way to get rid of them."

"But here we are," Taisiya said. "In the middle of the taiga. Just the three of us, and a trillion mosquitoes."

"Yes," Lilia said. "And I am still waiting to hear why."

"What if I told you," Gleb said, "that at the center of the state—right at the center of everything that is doing all of this—there is a zero-day vulnerability? A vulnerability we can exploit to change the whole country, once and for all?"

"I would ask you why you haven't used it."

"We'll get one shot. But once we do, we need to be able to see inside the system."

"You know," Lilia said, "that the dioramas aren't only about *seeing* inside the system."

The white rose. Perfect and colorless as a hole in the world.

I don't know why I bought it for you, really. I was just passing by the florist and saw it in the window.

"We know. They are about being able to make *changes*. That's what we need. Insurance. Control. Not only a window in, but also levers. Can the dioramas really give us that?"

"Not on their own. They are keys. They need to be hooked up to the right program on the right machine," Lilia said, "and then they will give you not just a real-time model of the network's activity, but the ability to influence it as well."

"To put thoughts in someone's head."

I don't know why I bought it for you, really. I was just passing by the florist and saw it in the window.

"Yes."

"And what happens if someone else gets them?" Taisiya asked. "Could they reverse engineer them?"

"Not easily," Lilia said.

"What if they had Palmer as well?"

"Then—maybe. Maybe if they had engineers that were good enough. If they could see both ends of the connection. If they could hook him and the diorama up to the right equipment. Maybe, if they already knew what they were looking for. I don't know. I think it would take them a long time. But having him would speed things up. Where is this zero-day vulnerability?"

"In the mind of the President," Gleb said. "Not at this moment, but soon."

"What do you mean, 'soon'? You can't get in there."

"No, we can't. But we've infiltrated his replacement build."

"His replacement could be decades away."

"No. That is what we believed too. But we have a mole in the palace, feeding us information. The President is dying.

This latest iteration was flawed. The blank is rejecting his neural connectome. The President has weeks to live. Maybe less. If it's less—"

"I need the dioramas," Lilia said. "If you want all of this quickly, I need those. If I have to rebuild it all, it will take longer than weeks. I need the dioramas, and I need to know that Palmer is safe. You need to help him."

Gleb looked at Taisiya.

"I can't promise anything," she said.

"You said Palmer managed to get out of London without getting himself killed. And with the dioramas?"

"Yes."

"You must know where he is, then. You can find him, get the dioramas, and help him get away from whoever else is after him."

"We don't know the details of that part of the operation," Gleb said. "All we know is the part we play. That's the way we keep each other safe."

"But you know about the plot to replace the President."

"We know because we needed to tell it to you," Gleb said. "To convince you to help us. If it weren't for that reason, they never would have let us in on it."

"We work on our aspect of the problem," Taisiya said. "The rest of it is out there in the dark."

The taiga. Bands of impenetrable forest—and a dozen clearings in the trees, each with its little 3D-printed izba. Or hundreds of them. Or thousands. In each, a conversation happening. Or people bent over computers. People taking people into the izbas, people digging graves, people handing out rifles—and the walkers lumbering through the trees, the larch and the cedars, the birch groves and the bogs, connecting it all.

"So you don't know who is paying for all of this? Who is really behind it all?"

"That isn't our part," Gleb said.

"It could be our enemies. Someone who wants nothing more than to tear our state apart."

"You sound like a propaganda feedstream," Taisiya said.

"It could be anyone."

"We have confidence," Gleb said. "In what we do and why we are doing it."

"So what happens when you use the zero-day vulnerability? What does it give you?"

"A chance," said Taisiya, "to destroy *autocracy*. To tear it apart from the inside."

15

THE PRESIDENT / NIKOLAI
The Federation

The President stood naked at his window, looking out at the sea. The waves came in slow and viscous, as if his sped-up perception were holding them back, delaying their progress across the surface of the sea.

After the sea had been denuded of boats all the way to the horizon to keep them away from the presidential residence, he had missed their white sails. But eventually, he stopped noticing their absence.

Today, the memory of them came back. The way a triangle of sail in the distance was suspended against water of no color there were words for. If you looked through binoculars, you could see the press of wind on the sail, the boat's furious wake. To the people in it, it was tearing across the water. From a distance, it was as motionless as if cast in glass, on glass waves.

That was what the waves were like now—molten glass, puddling themselves onto the shore.

There was a void in his vision—a tattered curtain of black in the periphery of his right eye, the world torn away. There were filaments of it elsewhere: dark threads twitching as he tried to focus on the silent sea beyond the window's reinforced glass.

What he should do is take a walk on the beach. Like the walks he had taken when he was a child, when his body had not been this body and he had wandered the field of wave-smoothed pebbles, listening to the hiss of water as it swept over them and then retreated, sucked down through the spaces between the stones and back out into itself. He had looked up into a sky where gulls balanced their wingtips in the passing air.

But if he walked on the beach now, it would be with a dozen security guards, ministers, and other hangers-on watching him. He would feel the impatience of these people who could not enjoy themselves in his presence. How they stood there, arms awkwardly crossed or dangling at their sides like dead things, waiting for him to grow tired of the beach and return to his palace so they could go about their business.

Their presence was always reluctant. Until they were allowed to leave, they had to stand with obedient and waiting expressions on their faces. Expressions it pained them to maintain. You could read that pain—not on their blank and practiced faces, but in the unnatural way they held their arms. They could never decide what to do with their arms. They crossed them across their chests, or hid them behind their backs, or let them hang at their sides—but whatever they chose, it was always wrong.

They had power. They were ministers, top-level security experts, men and women chosen and rewarded by the state.

But in your presence, they were vulnerable. Their own power relied on your absence. The enjoyment of their lives—lives you had granted to them—depended on being away from you.

The door opened. Nikolai came into the room and made his agonizingly slow approach toward the President's naked form.

Nikolai did not wince. His face was empty of disgust or pity.

The President admired that self-control. He knew what Nikolai saw: the marks of impending death on his flaking, reddened flesh, the bloody star of his separating iris. He had spent the morning in machines, being scanned, on Nikolai's orders.

And he knew the doctor saw not just the outward decay—this strange uncoupling of mind from body that was necrotizing his flesh—but also the errors inside. The malfunctioning of tendon, fluid, neuron, and bone.

The President pushed at a loose tooth with his tongue.

Nikolai's hands were not awkwardly idle. They had purpose. They were the hands of a healer. Whatever was going on in Nikolai's mind, the President trusted his hands.

"The results are not good," Nikolai slurred from the slow space of his unaugmented world. "The rejection is progressing faster than I had anticipated."

"How long?"

"Weeks, at the most—and I am afraid they may not be good weeks. We need to back up your connectome today, then every day from here forward, to have the most recent possible archive."

The void in the President's vision covered half of Nikolai's dutiful face, consuming the doctor. A filament of darkness severed Nikolai's arm. The President imagined, for a moment, the darkness consuming the doctor. As if he could give his own death to the doctor, blot Nikolai out of the world instead of himself. He would do it, of course. Without a moment's hesitation.

There was no sense in wishing it on someone else. It was *he* who was being torn apart. The President himself.

He wanted, for the first time in a long while, to make small talk. To ask Nikolai something normal. About his family, maybe.

But questions from him about people's families always sounded like a threat. "How is your family?" from the President meant "I can do whatever I like to your family. I know where they are and how to get to them."

The truth was different. He knew little about Nikolai's family. He knew they were in Italy, in some villa Nikolai had managed to avoid having sanctioned by strictly following his Hippocratic obligations.

If something ever needed to be done to Nikolai's family, it would be done by someone else. The President did not need to know where the people he'd decided to kill lived, or what their names were, or how they had been killed.

The power of someone like Krotov was the kind that required knowing the details of Nikolai's family life. The power to *not* know such things was the kind of power the President had: to destroy others in perfect ignorance of the details.

"Do you walk on the beach, Nikolai?" the President said.

The expression on Nikolai's face was startled—almost guilty. Even simple questions were a threat.

"I used to walk on the beach," the President said, too

impatient to wait for Nikolai's answer. "Right here. When I was a boy." He had wanted to say a *real* boy. "This was where my family came in the summers. At first, we rented a house. The same house every summer. Then, when my father became more successful, we bought the house.

"You can't see the beach I walked on from this window, but it is directly below us. I spent hours there some days. My parents loved things I did not love. My mother loved to be in boats on the water. My father loved to hunt and fish. What I loved was to be near the water. To walk on that beach. I loved the way the water hissed down through the stones under the white sun. You could imagine it going all the way down, right to the core of a world as porous as a sponge. I used to wonder how the sea did not drain away through all the holes. When it came time to build my summer residence, I told them to build it here, near the house where I spent those summers as a boy."

"An understandable choice," Nikolai said.

"A terrible choice. When I arrived at the palace for the first time, I discovered no one had told them that the house on the shore was my boyhood home. So they tore it down. They ripped apart the hillside it stood on and flung their construction trash onto the beach where I had spent so many summer days.

"I made them clean the beach up, but for the rest—nothing could be done. The home where I spent my childhood summers was gone. Our family had sold the house long ago. The people it belonged to were no one, so the state stripped it from them. I never mentioned the house to anyone, so how could they have known it was important? There was no one to hold responsible but myself."

"Still," Nikolai said, "it seems so clumsy."

"That is the way of everything here," the President said. "No one asks. They are too afraid. They simply act—stupidly. And then it is too late, and there is nothing left to do except punish people for their mistakes."

Nikolai was examining his back. The President could feel a cool instrument—perhaps the tip of a pen—along a shoulder blade.

"I can almost imagine where the old house was—here inside this one. I swear that the edge of where my bed was when I was a boy overlaps where my bed is now. And the old concrete staircase, the cracked staircase that wound down the hill to the sea, crosses through the grand staircase in the new hall."

"The ghost of a house," Nikolai said, "inside the palace."

"Yes."

Moving in front of him, Nikolai shone a penlight into his eye. "How is your vision?"

"Deteriorating." He did not want to talk about the void. What did it matter? All of this would be over soon enough. There would be a new body, a new start.

"You were here for the last transition, Nikolai," the President said. "I have faith you will handle this one just as well."

The half of Nikolai not sliced away by darkness said, "We will take more care this time. No more augmentations. Human flesh was made to house a human mind. Although they are artificially created, the blanks are human flesh."

"You were against these innovations from the beginning. The sped-up mental processes, the other 'improvements' I wanted."

"I would have been more cautious."

Nikolai slurred those words with half of his face cut away by the void. Again, it was so easy for the President to imagine that Nikolai was the one dying. Or the entire world—the sea outside the window, the horizon cut away, the dark growing until it took everything.

It was a comforting thought—the world dying, instead of him.

Krotov was in his office, a sub-basement room with a feedstream terminal on the wall that mimicked a saltwater fish tank. Or perhaps it was a stream from a real reef. Nikolai had never asked which. As he watched, an octopus strolled stealthily along the bottom, turned into a coral, turned into sand, turned into itself again—all as casually as thinking.

There was a dead seagull on the table in front of Krotov.

"Weeks, then. Well, Nikolai, we've been ready for this. The blank is prepared, the transition plan is in place. I would have liked a little more time to set the information stage—more rumors of foreign interference, some kind of diplomatic skirmish, a spy caught. Those are nice touches. But anyway, we've made sure the people will accept what we tell them. Or act as if they accept it. It's all the same thing in the end."

The seagull's open eye reflected the ceiling's recessed LEDs. Krotov turned it belly up. Its head flopped on a limp neck. For a moment its dark eye met Nikolai's.

With his thumbs, Krotov massaged the bird's chest. Then he dug his thumbs into the feathers and split it open.

There was no blood. Inside was an articulated framework filled with wires.

"You remember I once joked that even the seagulls needed a permit to be here?" asked Krotov. "Well, we caught this one on the beach this morning. It was acting strangely. One of my people netted it with a patrol drone."

A feather had detached itself from the gull. Nikolai picked it up from the table. It was real enough to fool him.

"A clever observation platform," Krotov said. "I like it. It has its disadvantages, of course. The main one is that it's quite limited in the kind of data it can collect. It's not like you can have a seagull looking in someone's bedroom window or walking through the kitchen. I imagine the real advantage, though"—he stripped the feathery sheath of the bird away, baring the whole mechanism to view—"is that it can record what it sees or hears, then fly out of range before broadcasting back to its operators. That keeps us from picking up a signal."

The limp husk of feathers lay on the table; the empty hole in its head where its eye had been pointed at the ceiling.

"It makes you paranoid of everything," Nikolai said.

"You should be, Nikolai. Total connectivity is total vulnerability. I can't step on a beetle without picking it up and digging around in its guts to be sure it's really organic. Paranoia is the only sane response to a world composed of keyholes through which the eyes of our enemies may peer at any time. How is our President?"

Krotov did not ask questions to gain new information; he asked them to weigh your response against other information he already had, other calculations.

"He is deteriorating very quickly. His mental functioning will begin to suffer soon, if it hasn't already. We'll have to begin scanning the updates for corruptions."

"Corruptions?"

"It's a feedback loop now between the body and the mind. This kind of dissolution will cause damage to his neural structure, which will damage his tissues, which will cause more damage to the connectome. And then there is a chance—I think it is slim, at the moment, but it is there—that he will suffer a fatal event before we are prepared for the transition."

Nikolai used the word "we." There was no "we." What did he know about the preparations Krotov had made for the transition? Nothing. There was a dance already begun. Rumors put into place, an identity formed for the blank, documents forged, but more than that—actors in position to act the parts of mother, father, daughter, friend who had watched his rise, adoring professor to speak about his talents. Generated clips of him living his life, whole archives of photos.

And on the other hand, there must already be memorial feedstreams prepared, speeches polished eulogizing the President's current version.

The medical practice was simple in comparison.

"And what will you do?"

"Whatever is necessary," Nikolai said. "I will be standing by until he is back online. Until all of it is stabilized."

"I mean now. This moment."

"I thought I would take a walk along the beach."

"That sounds like a fine idea," Krotov said. "But if you see any disloyal-looking seagulls, report them to me immediately."

The beach was at the base of a steep bluff. The residence loomed on the top of the hill, ugly despite its enormous cost and the employment of the country's best architects. Or because of those facts.

The beach was of mottled greenish stone rolled in the water for eons. It was not ruined, even by the proximity of the state's architectural monstrosity. As Nikolai walked along it, under the white blaze of a late-summer sun, he imagined the boy who had spent the hot days here, staring out over the water.

The boy would have watched sailboats close to shore, swimmers in and just beyond the breakers. For a moment, as if the President had managed to stamp the traces of his own memories into Nikolai's mind, Nikolai imagined the crooked concrete stairs leading down to the beach and the little house they led to.

A gone world, the antithesis of the pompous white staircase that now ascended the bluff, the bloated façade of windows blanked by mirrored glass.

Overhead, a gyre of gulls banked and tilted their bodies in an onshore breeze.

At the end of the beach, where an outcropping of cliff pushed out into the sea, Nikolai took a black pebble from his pocket. He placed it on a ledge of rock.

There was nothing unusual about the pebble, except that it was not from here.

16

ELMIRA
The City-State

On the plane from London, Elmira's mind had returned many times to the university courtyard she had looked down into. To the sapling, with its leaves turning yellow. The tree that understood autumn had arrived. That had gotten that information before she had. Before anyone had. Had known it. In its roots? On the surface of its bark? What did it mean for a tree to *know* a thing?

She remembered the screens of the terminals the students had gathered around. The fire there: a building burning. The way the students gathered around the screens as if the fire were giving off real warmth.

Now she understood what they had been looking at: Rationalization's first recorded failure. The end of a PM government. The burning of the Parliament building housing the mind of a PM, in one of the little republics that once had been under the Federation's power, but now was an unstable country all its own.

On the flight back, at the airport, people passed along rumors. The little republic's PM had gone mad. It had raised energy prices again and again until it *caused* the revolution that destroyed it.

"I heard," someone said, "that it was raising prices until they matched the real cost of energy. Not for the energy companies, but for the *planet itself.*"

"I heard," someone else said, into their terminal, "that it's a Western plot to undermine developing countries. The PMs they gave to those countries were *designed* to fail. Then, when the revolution comes, the Western countries can occupy them in the name of peacekeeping and steal their resources."

"I heard it was terrorists," someone said.

But perhaps that person had not even been talking about the PM. Someone was always talking about terrorists, somewhere.

On the feedscreens the pundits reassured everyone: *an isolated case*. And then, after a few hours, the tone of the broadcasts changed. They did not talk anymore about isolation. Instead, they talked about *incompatibility*. About how the extension of rationalization had gone too far. Rationalization might work in the West, the pundits said, but there were countries out there that were not ready for it, the talking heads insisted. The Republic was one of those. This failure had been caused by hastiness, by overreach, by thinking that "we" (and the meaning of that "we" kept shifting) could push our values on a world "not ready" for development.

Recently, the streams had begun referring to countries without PM governance as "pre-rationalized."

"They say it was radicals in their own government who caused it," someone said.

Nowhere was it said, on the feedscreens, that there might be something wrong with rationalization itself. But Elmira sensed that conclusion in the faces of people watching. In the faces that looked the most tired. In the *working another double shift* faces. In the *trying to raise a child in this "rationalized" world* faces.

She was so used to masking her own emotion that, perhaps, no one would have seen it in her face. But it was there.

Let it burn.

This phrase kept recurring in her mind: let it burn. Let the fire spread. Over the whole globe, if that was what it took.

Whatever it was, this rolling collapse of systems, it had not yet reached Istanbul. But she prayed it would.

Let it burn.

"They say they would like to help us," she overheard someone saying, "but the government doesn't have the resources right now."

Somehow, there were never enough resources to help everyone. Somehow, after rationalization, *that* had not changed. The same systems, replicating themselves through human or nonhuman means.

If she were successful in her work, if all of them were successful, they might bring down one government. But the other rotten systems would remain.

But now she thought, *Maybe not. Maybe the fire would spread instead. Maybe everything* could *be changed.*

She was tired. And tired of thinking about all of this. She clenched and unclenched her left hand, massaged her palm.

Maybe Palmer would be smart enough not to be picked up by her systems for a few days. What she could use, more than anything else, was rest. A day, two days, to think. To be here, in Istanbul, without the constant hiss of the voice in her ear.

Elmira rode the Tekray along a Marble Sea glaucous and undulating in the blue-shifted light. The hives of cell towers beyond the southern boundaries of the city tessellated past. A few windows were already lit up. It was a cold morning with a salt wind off the sea. The tree in the London courtyard was right: autumn was coming to the world.

There was already a line at the immigration center. The hopefuls blew into their hands against the morning cold. The City-State of Istanbul had announced a new citizenship lottery, with the promise of rationalized benefits—pensions, insurance, pay minimums, safety nets.

Her parents had stood in those lines. Wrapped up against the wind and the cold, holding umbrellas to keep off the rain, holding umbrellas to keep off the sun. They stood in those lines for years, existing just outside the City-State's boundaries, in the Limited-Governance Area, where the air tasted of cement dust. They had lost their own country, so they stood in line with everyone else who had lost a country.

That was how it was. One day you had your own country. The next day you were a refugee. You were in a line, waiting to be someone again. To be *legal* again. Not to be nothing.

You could spend your whole life waiting.

Her father had. He had spent his days either working or in line. He had spent his evenings talking about the country he had lost—lost because he had fought to change it. Elmira's father and mother had fought together.

Other parents—local parents—talked of local things. Here-and-now things. The things you talked about when you had a country. But Elmira's parents talked of the lost past. They talked of their days at the barricades, of battles with riot police on the square, of the kitchen planning sessions. They talked of collective action.

Her mother talked of Zoya Velikanova picking up a tear gas canister, walking calmly over to a police van, and throwing it into the cab. She talked of being there when Zoya lost an eye from a rubber bullet. Elmira's mother had written her memoirs, which were less her own story than a paraphrasing of *The Forever Argument*.

Even when Zoya's lover Yuri was killed, Elmira's parents had stayed with the movement. They had hung on. But then others started going as well—this one murdered in an elevator, that one beaten to death in a robbery, this one killed in a car accident, that one who just left home one day and never came back.

Finally, they fled.

Her father kept returning to moments in his past, trying to figure out where it had all gone wrong. They had thought, for so long, that they would win one day. One day the wars would end. One day they would elect the leaders they needed. The leaders they deserved. The system should have collapsed already, but it hadn't. It was stronger than any of them had thought.

No matter. One day it would come tumbling down. It had to. It *had to*. The refugees would flood home. The time was right around the corner—no regime could last forever. And their people were too smart for this. Too smart!

And then one day, standing in line waiting, he slumped to his knees and died.

When their identity cards came, Elmira and her mother found out they had not been granted asylum. They were given nothing more than an opportunity for "paid residence." The authorities had decided that their returning to their own country presented no "immediate threat to their safety." There was no appeal.

"I waited for years for them to listen to us," Elmira's mother said. "And finally I figured out they weren't interested in listening. They were interested in what they could get from us. Cheap labor on the gray market, for nothing in return."

For Elmira's mother, paid residence meant an extra ten floors scrubbed a month for her own fee. And an extra thirty rooms dusted for her daughter's.

It wasn't the money that was the worst of the problem—it was what you had to do to get it. It was how tired the extra work made you at the end of the week. It was how many times you couldn't afford to rest, how many Saturdays were spent working, how many Sundays. It was not walking in the park with your child. It was not laughing with them in the evening.

It was what all of that took from you. The years it took off the end of your life. And the years it took along the way. Her mother stopped writing her memoirs. She stopped speaking of the past. Nostalgia took energy. Memory came at a cost.

She never stopped paying for losing her country. The cost

was so high that she could no longer afford to return from exile, even in memory.

Elmira didn't want to go home yet to her cell, barren of anything. On a branch-line platform, she bought a *simit* from a vendor and sat down on the bench to feed the sparrows haunting the station. She tore tiny pieces off the ring of sesame-spangled bread for the fierce, fat little birds. They battled one another for position and twisted their little heads, regarding her with one glistening sable eye and then the other, always eager for more.

She bought another simit ring and settled on the bench again.

Her mother's last words to her had been "You look tired. You should sleep more."

And Elmira was tired. Because she had taken up the burden. You see what your parents do for you, and it pushes you. You study harder, you work more. You'll always be aliens here, with the language you speak in the kitchen a remnant from a lost place. With the charge always due at the end of the month for the "maintenance of an alien presence," as the City-State put it in its insulting bureaucratic language.

And you weren't even worthy of pity. Your country wasn't the one that was being attacked—it was the aggressor. It was one of the states making the world worse. Even though your family had been *victims* of all that, had fled that, they were not the same as those who had fled from the wars your country started. Why didn't you go back and fight? If all of you stood up together, the President and his entire system would fall, wouldn't they?

No use telling them her parents had tried that—again, and

again, and again. Her mother had been there on the square with Zoya when half the movement was killed in a single day.

When her mother told that story it always sounded like an accusation. What have you done, Elmira?

Even if Elmira knew it wasn't meant that way, it felt like it was—because what *had* she done?

And so Elmira acted.

In the end, it was not hard to find them. Hang around the places where the other émigrés gathered to talk politics, and eventually they found you.

"Would it bother you," the man who found her asked, "to work your whole life, to do terrible things, but never know if any of it made a difference?" he asked.

She shrugged. "Isn't that just—life?"

"You'll do well with us."

Elmira took a few bites of the simit ring. It was long past dawn now. Commuters were showing up on the platform. But she felt no need to leave. She had been moving forward with such speed all these months. Doing, not thinking. Surviving, not living. Now, finally, she had a moment to pause.

When her mother died, two months ago, she had not stopped. She'd scattered her mother's ashes in the Marble Sea, where the ashes of millions had been scattered over the centuries, and kept going.

It felt like the new movement was getting closer. She wanted to be a part of that. It felt like the killing would be worth it: the fear, the midnight wakeups, evacuating flats and on the move again. She had never been sorry for the killing before—it was an action, at least.

One of the sparrows on the platform had an artificial foot.

Its brown dinosaur leg was grafted to a construct of delicate carbon fiber struts and miniature talons of hardened glass. The foot flexed and grasped exactly like its other foot of flesh and blood.

Who would take the time to do such a thing? This little piece of kindness, like a gap torn in the net of injustice.

Her mother's hospital bills had consumed any amount of money she could scrape together. Medical care, free for any citizen, was a disaster for "paid residents" like them.

Who decided these things? When the PM was installed and the City-State rationalized, Elmira had believed things would change. But they did not—not really. The fees decreased, a few more cases were granted asylum. There was a softening at the edges, but nothing was really different. Not for them.

"Their system isn't for us," her mother said. "We were left out of their calculations from the start."

"The PMs are supposed to promote *human flourishing*."

"The question is who gets to be a *human*. That has always been the question. You look tired. You should sleep more."

Those were her last words to Elmira. She died hours later, alone, while Elmira was chasing down a lead.

At the hospital, she retrieved her mother's possessions—the few things she'd brought to the hospital with her. Documents and a few changes of clothes and Zoya's book, *The Forever Argument*.

The others in Elmira's cell had all read the book. Elmira had never opened its covers.

It was difficult to burn a thing. She had to go to two stores before she found lighter fluid and a lighter.

Finding a secluded place was even more difficult: it took riding the Tekray to its terminus, and then walking twenty minutes or more, past the last angler, to a piece of waste ground along the Marble Sea—shattered wooden boats and bird shit, an algae-slimed seawall. There she burned the book down to a hunk of charred pages. The wind swirled the ashes around her.

Riding back on the Tekray she had reeked of ash and kerosene. The smell was old, nostalgic. But that was wrong: it was not a smell from her own childhood. It was older than that.

She kept stumbling forward. Kept doing what she was told. But it had lost its meaning. She had believed she was doing all of this to make a change in the world—but that hadn't been it at all.

It was nothing but the floor she was scrubbing for her mother. It was the rooms she was dusting for her mother, to make sure she did her share. Elmira had taken up the burden of revolution not to change the world, but for her parents. For her father, holding his head in his hands and wondering what could have been different. For her mother, scrubbing floors for the rich because her labor was cheaper than maintaining a machine to do it.

Now that her mother was gone, none of it was worth it anymore. She had believed it was her fight, but it was not. Her country was lost to her. All countries were lost to her.

The tiny cyborg sparrow poked one of its comrades in the butt, startling it into dropping its bread, then seized the prize and flew off, triumphant, with a hunk of simit half the size of its head clasped in its beak.

Someone had taken the time to replace a wounded bird's

foot, just so it could do that most important thing of all—live. Squabble and bicker with its tribe, chatter aimlessly, make more life.

That was worth doing—not taking life but prolonging it. That was what Zoya had done: fought for life. And that was what her mother and her father and all the others had been trying to do—they had been trying to prolong life.

No more. I'm finished, and I'll tell them. I am finished.

The connection crackled to life in her ear.

We have him.

17

NURLAN
The Republic

Nurlan dove into the bushes at the sound of the approach of a group of men. They whooped and yelled as he lay curled on his side, clutching his terminal to his stomach. Their booted feet were five meters from his head. They all wore the same new, black technical boots. Their accents told him they were from the villages. They drifted into local dialects he couldn't understand.

They shifted their rifles from one shoulder to another and laughed, passing a bottle around. Then one of them fired an automatic rifle into the sky. The sound was deafening. Nurlan almost cried out.

They were looking for people dressed like him. He would be beaten if they found him. Maybe killed. The night's killing certainly wasn't over yet. The killing might not be over for days, as faction battled faction for power and the Republic struggled to right itself.

Gunfire rattled in the distance. Then a loud thump. A tank shell? A mortar round? A drone, dropping a grenade on some rival group?

Part of the burning Parliament building collapsed. Flame-shadows quivered and twitched on the ground through the web of branches and leaves. There were other explosions from more distant parts of the city.

As he had run from the building, he saw a thing worse than the fire itself: the walker, climbing the side of the building through the fire. Climbing, invulnerable, through the flames.

What had Nurlan done? What had he saved? The Parliament was burning, the government had fallen. The people he had been in a room with less than an hour ago must be dead. Of fire, of smoke, or bashed to a pulp by that black, enormous thing scaling the walls.

Why had he put himself at risk? Why bother shutting it down? The men on the square would have burned the building down anyway. The PM would have been destroyed anyway. Why hadn't Hazal just shown him the way out instead?

We will meet, and I will tell you everything. But for that to happen, you must survive

Nurlan had spent his entire life trying to avoid being at the center of anything. Now here he was, a block from a burning building, and *he* was the one who had brought the government down. Him! The parliamentary staffer so quiet he could be in a room for an hour before anyone noticed him.

Before Hazal, he hadn't wanted anything except to go unnoticed at work, eat a good meal in the evening, have enough in his account to keep the mortgage paid on his apartment.

At first, Hazal was like a part of himself: a relationship so natural that he didn't have to think of it much. What she was doing was important. She had been out of the country for years. He'd caught hints, suggestions of her work, but she could not tell him the details.

But he was used to that. In his job, in the hallways and the offices of Parliament, hints and suggestions were everywhere. And he had staffed more than a few secret meetings in which there were more than just hints.

He knew she was a part of what they called "the Apparatus"—that mix of security and intelligence organizations that played all the ugly, necessary games of chess with the Republic's enemies, internal and external. While the PM and its vestigial Parliament kept the surface running, the Apparatus monitored groups like these men with their boots so close to Nurlan's head.

But Hazal had not wanted to talk about her work. Instead, she told him about her childhood in the mountains. About riding her first horse when she was five years old. She told him about the way winter came at three thousand meters. One morning you woke up and there was a skin of ice on the lake as thick as window glass. You could hold a piece of it up and turn the morning sun into rainbows. Then it was time to move the herd into the lower valleys. The snow would not be far behind.

She gave him that memory—described it so clearly that he could remember it as his own. He wondered whether, in his city life, he had ever noticed the day when a season changed. Or cared? There was a day when you realized you should have brought a coat to work. That was all.

The men walked away, laughing and drinking.

He looked at the terminal's empty battery, the red outline on a black screen. More than safety, what he wanted was to get the terminal plugged in at his apartment and power it up so he could talk to Hazal. So he could tell her he was okay. He was alive. They would see one another once all of this was over.

Nurlan pulled himself up into a crouch and listened. After he left the park he would be only a few blocks from home—but the blocks around the government buildings were enormous marble and concrete plazas. Nowhere to hide. Bands of men like the ones who had come close to catching him were everywhere.

His tie was already gone—somewhere back there in the building, maybe ashes now. Which was worse? The dark suit jacket he still wore, or the white shirt underneath? The white shirt was a target—one of the men might take a shot at it for little reason, seeing it in the dark. But he decided the suit jacket was worse—it was like a declaration, here in the center of the city, that he had been part of the government they hated.

He took his jacket off. Then he took off his belt as well. Real leather, with a silver buckle. There would be looters. He dropped his belt to the ground.

He tucked the terminal under his shirt. He scuffed the shine from his shoes. Now he could be anyone. A shop clerk trapped down here when the unrest began, maybe.

Flames poured from the upper stories of Parliament. Near the edge of the square was a fire engine hit by protesters with Molotov cocktails. Its burned frame stood on melted tires, under its blackened ladder. A dead man lay on the ground near it.

George. Asel. Atabek. Jyldyz. The old lion Erlis Jeenbaev. Were they all dead? Or had they found their own ways out somehow?

Nurlan walked into the darkness of the park. He walked swiftly, with his head down. He fought the urge to run. Running would make him a target.

WE WILL MEET, AND I WILL TELL YOU EVERYTHING. BUT FOR THAT TO HAPPEN, YOU MUST SURVIVE

They had agreed, in those first days of texting back and forth, not to exchange pictures. That was what other people did. Their relationship, they decided, would not be like other people's.

After all, it had not started like other people's. It had started with her sending a text to a wrong number on a secure device.

Nurlan had taken a new building communications terminal from the distribution office. The person who'd had it before had not deleted their comms key. The next morning, sitting down to eat a cereal bar on a bench in the corridor, he had received her first message:

ARE YOU STILL READING ME?

WHO IS THIS? he'd typed in response.

WHO IS THIS?

That was how it began. It grew into a series of back-and-forth texts on the little nothings of work and life. No more than banter, for the first weeks. But he could feel a tension growing in himself. Soon enough, every time he locked the secure terminal into its charging station in the tech room, it was as meaningful as a kiss goodnight.

He had time, in the evenings, to think of the next day. Time for anticipation. And he knew Hazal felt the same. She never asked for his personal terminal's comms key, and he had never offered it. It was understood between them that the limits on their relationship—the refusal to exchange pictures, the few hours a day of texting—would make the moment when they stepped into each other's lives more perfect.

Several times, Nurlan heard groups of men coming and stepped off the path into the dark under the trees. Once, he found another man hiding there: a man in a suit jacket like the one Nurlan had taken off. The man's face was streaked with soot. He was bleeding from a cut on his head.

They said nothing to one another, but Nurlan helped the man stanch the bleeding. He showed the man how to keep pressure on the wound and gave him a clean handkerchief from his pocket.

He'd seen this man before. On the Parliament floor, in a hallway, in the cafeteria. Somewhere. This man, or a man exactly like him.

The fighting was not in the park. And most of the gunshots came from the south, away from Nurlan's apartment.

Nurlan was walking through the amusement park section now. The skeleton of the Ferris wheel was blurred by smoke. The horizon glowed a dull orange, although the sun had been down for hours. The Parliament was no longer the only building on fire.

He reminded himself not to run. Coming out of the park

he crossed a street empty of cars. A block away, a bus was sideways across the road, its windows spiderwebbed. A block away in the other direction, a dump truck obstructed the street.

When he was in the middle of the road, a voice called out for him to stop. Now he ran. There was a shot, and then another. Aimed at him? He could not tell. Then he was across.

In the dead space between two apartment buildings, Nurlan stopped to catch his breath.

He had heard that adrenaline made people tireless. That fear helped people perform feats of amazing strength. That was certainly not true for him. Fear had drained all the strength from his legs. He slid down the wall and sat on the dirty ground between two battered garbage bins.

There were sirens and the rattle of guns. But the city was no louder than it might be on a holiday, when contraband fireworks popped overhead and fire trucks rushed from incident to incident, stabbing at their horns to clear people from the road.

In the buildings around him he could see the dim glow of terminals and home feedscreens behind drawn curtains and blinds. *They think they can keep watching, but they are in the middle of it now. There is nowhere left to watch from.*

He got himself to his feet. His legs were shaking. His hands too. Not far now—through the battered yard between these buildings, then another block and he was home.

He would charge the terminal before the city lost power, let Hazal know he was safe. And behind his own barricaded door, he *would* be safe. He was no one. He had been, by accident, at the center of things. But that was only for a moment. Now he was no one again.

That was where he would stay: on the periphery of it all. There would be a new government, no different from the old one. There would be a new PM, or not. Whatever they chose to do, there would be a need to staff the new Parliament. He would be called up. He would return to his job.

No one would ever know what he had done. All he had to do was live through this moment, this chaos between this government and the next.

He crossed the courtyard, staying in the deep shadow of one of the buildings, away from the security lights that lit up a little playground's over-loved equipment and a shabby common garden.

The next street glittered under the streetlamps. Broken glass. The shopfronts here were looted. There was a clothing store he couldn't remember the name of, a terminal store, a bakery. There were clothes in the street. What he thought was another corpse turned out to be a mannequin.

There was a strange sound. Nurlan stopped in the shadow of a building's torn eaves.

A horse's hooves. Approaching from his left. A horse at a walk.

It came down the middle of the street in the cold white of the streetlamp LEDs. A horse and rider. The horse was a sorrel, tall and broad chested and shaggy, its head turning from side to side. The rider was slumped, unmoving, in the saddle. Asleep?

The man was dressed in black, like all the men who had flooded into the city, taking their orders, their alcohol, and some money to bring a country down. The top of the man's head was gone. Everything above the jawbones, gone. His dead hands still held the reins as the horse walked calmly down the center of the street.

His grin was a pink streak of bone.

The horse's hooves crunched on shattered safety glass as it crossed in front of him. Nurlan pushed his back against the wall to keep himself upright as his knees gave out.

Once the horse and the thing it carried were a few hundred meters away, he ran.

He was across. On this side of the street, nothing had been touched. At the entrance of his own building, he punched in his code.

He did not take the elevator: he took the stairs, the dismal concrete well of stairs he usually avoided, filled with his neighbors' cooking smells. Someone had a feedscreen blaring.

He was in his own hallway. At his own door. He fumbled the entry glyph twice, then managed to get it right on the third try and went inside.

He was safe now.

After everything that had happened it was strange to see the order of his own apartment. Its neatness was disturbing. As if the person who lived here were hiding something.

He crossed the eating nook and set the terminal into his charger.

It was forbidden to take the terminal from the Parliament building.

He began to laugh—a weird, light sound in his chest, more like a cough. What Parliament building?

The screen blinked as the charging icon came on. But it did not settle into the steady green pulse that indicated it was charging. Instead, it went bright white, then black.

The dead black of a bricked terminal.

He heard himself say "no" aloud.

He had lost her.

No. I cannot find Hazal, but she can find me. And she will. She has to.

18

PALMER

The City-State

The men struggled to pull the thing from the Bosporus, thrusting long, hooked poles into the water from the deck of their boat. A third man gave hand signals to the boat's pilot, who inched the craft closer to the thing.

From where Palmer stood, looking through a small telescope, the thing they were trying to pull from the water was barely more than a shadow. It had loops on its outer edge that looked naturally formed but must have been engineered for the hooks. One of the men got a hook through one of them and pulled it up to the surface. It was a bloated trash-collecting pseudojellyfish. The Thames was full of them as well.

Its swollen body was filled with shapes. Garbage. Cups, a torn net of some kind, plastic floats and other marine debris, utensils.

The second man got a hook into it, and they began hauling

it up the ramped side of the boat. The men had it halfway over the gunwale when it began to slacken and deform.

On the boat deck behind them was a pile of limp, gelatinous pseudojellies like this one, but smaller. This one must have malfunctioned, continuing to collect garbage until it swelled to near bursting.

It tore open. One of the men worked with a net, trying to scoop as much as he could of the trash up over the gunwale and into the boat as the loop tore away and the thing slid back into the water, disintegrating. The trash it had consumed sank with its ripped form. It resurfaced in a widening spiral of utensils, bobbers, unidentifiable fragments. Seagulls plunged and rose over it, looking for a meal, but there was nothing organic to be had.

Now both the men were working with nets on long poles, trying to scoop as much debris as they could up onto the boat before the trash sank or drifted out of reach. The ragged shadow of the pseudojellyfish drifted a few meters below the surface, becoming trash like the trash it had gathered.

The safe house where Palmer watched through the telescope was on a small bluff looking out over the Bosporus where the throat of the strait widened. Through his telescope Palmer could make out, when the day was clear, a long expanse of open water to the north that he knew was the Black Sea.

He had expected the Black Sea to be dark. Sometimes it was, hinting at the bleak, anoxic voids of its depths. But most of the time its surface was a mirror of the sky above it and the light that splintered on its waves.

On the train, Palmer had received more instructions on

the old terminal they had given him. An address and a ticket for a ferry.

TAKE FERRY

SPEAK TO NO ONE ON BOARD

OUR AGENT WILL MEET YOU ON THE DOCK WHEN YOU DISEMBARK

When he arrived in Istanbul, the train station was filled with people. Autonomous police cameras loitered overhead, whirring down at times to get a second look at someone. They ignored him. It was a short but crowded walk to the quay, where he presented his ticket to a machine and boarded the autoferry up the Bosporus.

On the ferry, he had imagined the landing with dread. A jagged coast of roofs and minarets, the dock bustling with people waiting for ferry passengers or waiting for the ferry. A man on the pier, waiting for him with folded arms. A man who stood at the end of all this. Who would be the end of him. Anxiety clamped his hands to the rail.

Was this his life now? Imagining an enemy waiting for him on every pier?

He straightened his shoulders as the ferry came in to shore. He forced his grip on the rail to release itself and debarked with the others.

He stood for almost a minute on the dock, standing in bright sun, hot in the knit cap they had given him.

Now he was not afraid. Instead he had the giddy feeling that it would be Lilia who would meet him.

Palmer forced himself not to think this way either. It was worse than the fear he had felt before.

Finally, a man near the ferry terminal waved him over.

Palmer could not quite make out the man's face. Once he was almost within an arm's distance, he understood why. The man had some sort of distorter on. From a distance his face was as unremarkable as any face in a crowd. But up close it was like a face in an impressionist painting, its features no more than broad brushstrokes, resolving only with distance.

The smeared face triggered some deep loathing in Palmer, and fear.

How could he ever know what side anyone was on? Or even how many sides there might be? He had imagined two sides, but of course there could be many.

"Follow me," the man said, in a voice as electronically smudged as his face.

The man wore surgical gloves. This was not unusual—many people wore them in the city, or carried an antibacterial touchkey, or otherwise found ways to avoid the urban surfaces that might be coated with next year's global plague.

Palmer followed the man away from the dock. There was a flat area near the shore with a few benches and old mulberry trees. Beyond it, the streets rose steeply.

"I want to know where I am going," Palmer said.

"To a safe house."

"After that. I want to know where my destination is."

"Do you have them with you?"

What if he said he did not? How would that change things? Then something occurred to him.

"Do I have what with me?"

The man turned toward him.

Palmer wished he had not. The motion caused the features to writhe on the man's head. A mouth-scrawl said, "You know what."

"Do *you*?" Palmer asked.

"I know what I need to know."

"I have them."

"Good."

They went up a flight of stairs. The man turned a key in a metal door and gestured with a gloved hand.

"You must have a message for me," Palmer said.

The man placed the key in Palmer's hand. "No. That's all I have."

"How long will I be here?"

"You need to wait. That's all."

The man turned to go, but Palmer put a hand on his shoulder. "Listen—I just want to help. Whatever I can do to help Lilia, I'll do it. Tell them I want to help. I think I *can* help, if only someone will tell me what is going on. Where she is, and what I can do to get her back."

The man carefully removed Palmer's hand from his shoulder. "I'm sorry. I don't know anything else. I don't even know who you are. Or who this Lilia is."

"Please give them my message."

"I will."

The place was a studio apartment with a narrow bed, packaged foods in the refrigerator, clothes vaguely his size in the closet. There was the telescope for gazing out over the sea from behind a shield of one-way glass, a window as large as the wall. Beyond it the waters of strait and sea tantalized.

The waiting went on for days.

Finally, this morning, Palmer had been unable to wait any longer. He left the safe house a quarter hour after dawn.

He had expected something to stop him—a drone, perhaps, like the one that had adhered itself to the outside of his apartment window. But nothing came.

Wearing the knit cap, he walked down a narrow street that followed the curve of the bluff to a ragged harbor. Fishers were on the decks of their boats, tending to nets and machinery, faces blank with concentration.

Palmer looked for a place where he could get down to the water. The shore was crowded with houses, the water blocked off by shuttered restaurants and gates chained shut, guarded by salt-frosted, rusty manual locks. Finally, near the edge of the village, there was what one might call a beach. The cracked concrete disks of umbrella stands were scattered over an uninviting shelf of gravel. Across a narrow road was a convenience store, nothing more than a shack, really, but open even this early.

He sat on the gravel beach for a while. The morning was cold and misty. Maybe it would warm into a late-summer day, but at this hour autumn was in the air.

On the strait a massive autofreighter glided into the Black Sea. The ship was a tower of containers thirty stories high and looked as wide as the little town they had stored Palmer in. The misty smear of green lights on its starboard side left its calligraphy on the inside of his eyelids when he closed them.

The ship's name was written in Cyrillic letters.

Palmer had tried to learn that alphabet, tried to learn Lilia's language. He'd managed a few words, but every time he spoke it to her she would give him a pained smile. The smile of someone embarrassed by someone doing the wrong thing. She didn't want him to speak it.

So Palmer gave it up. The name on the ship remained unintelligible to him. A foreign ship, the size of a small city, making its way up the strait to the Black Sea. Getting closer to Lilia.

And Palmer stalled here. Going nowhere. Of use to no one. Palmer Blank.

What he needed was some kind of foothold on the situation. From there, possibilities would open up. He could find a way forward—to her, to helping her. To something. All he needed was for someone to talk to him, tell him what they wanted from him.

Whatever it was, he would do it. Whatever helped Lilia.

He felt a courage in himself that was like anger, or like a feeling he'd had as a child when he forced himself off the high diving platform despite his terror.

He crossed the road and walked into the convenience store. Not to buy anything. Simply to *do* something. From now on he was going to *do* things. He had already started: now all he needed to do was to keep up the momentum. To *act*.

Who knew what the motivations for an action were? Who could say? Once he had been walking by a florist's shop in London and had decided to buy Lilia a white rose. When had he made the decision? When he saw the rose? Maybe. But it felt as if the urge to buy the rose had preexisted that moment—as if he had been *led* to the rose. As if he had been looking for it. As if it had been inevitable.

Lilia had been so happy when she found it waiting for her on the table. He'd known, then, why he did it: to please her.

What else was that but love?

The little convenience store was nothing more than a shack, nailed together around a few narrow aisles of snacks—some new to him, others translated or transliterated versions of things he had seen before.

There was no one inside, but a cup of black tea in a pear-shaped glass was on the counter. He held a hand near it—it was still warm.

On a shabby monitor behind the counter, buildings burned.

At the back of the store was a display cooler filled with brightly colored energy drinks. Its feedstreaming glass hologrammed an ad at him of a man downing the contents of a bright yellow can. The hologram wiped its mouth and beckoned Palmer to join in with a motion of his head.

Palmer let his eyes wander over the contents of the cooler, not seeing anything he recognized. He had no way to buy anything, anyway. He turned and walked out.

Back in the safe house he drank tap water from the sink. He tried to read *The Forever Argument*. It was impossible to concentrate. He returned to the parts Lilia had underlined—to the trace of her there on the page:

From that moment, we understood that the state was everywhere. The state did not need to anticipate us: it was always with us. It shaped the mistakes we would make, and it was there to take us into its prisons when we made them.

The passage continued: *It was not only the security apparatus, watching us with eyes electronic and otherwise. It was also the way the state was built into us, containing our actions from the very beginning, defining the horizons of what we could think and be—and even of what we could see.*

Palmer thought, again, of the white rose.

A few days after he gave it to Lilia, they were at lunch. She started talking about some experiments, centuries ago. A story about how surgeons divided the brain hemispheres of people with severe epilepsy to stop the seizures—but this made it so that scientists could also tell one half of the brain things the other one did not know. Whisper in its ear, somehow, without the other half of the person hearing.

He couldn't quite understand the mechanism of it. There had been an experiment where they told one half of a man's brain to buy a Coke, and he got up and went to a machine and bought one. Then they asked the man why he'd done it, and he said he was thirsty.

Lilia said, "You see? He made up a reason for what he'd done. And he believed the reason. But it wasn't true at all. He hadn't bought that Coke because he was thirsty—he'd bought it *because he had been told to.*"

"But wouldn't he have sensed something was wrong? Wouldn't he have sensed he was lying to himself?"

"Would he?" Lilia asked. "They would even do experiments where they asked a person what they wanted to be. One half of the brain would answer 'engineer.' But if they showed the question to the other side of the brain—if they covered up one eye and showed the other one in secret—it would scrawl out 'priest.' As if there were *someone else in there.* A whole other person, with their own desires, trapped inside."

He remembered a feeling of unease. Lilia said, "I guess we never really know why we like the things we like or take the jobs we take, or how we end up where we are. Those experiments were no different, except that they made it obvious. I mean, why do you work where you work?"

"Oh, God. I ask myself that every day. Ask the computers. Maybe they know."

Palmer took the two dioramas out of the bag and set them on the table.

He had expected them to be the same as they had been before. They were not. His was no longer the ant farm: now it was an open sea. At the center of the sea was a sailing ship. It was hard to judge any distance, or progress, with nothing on any horizon, but the tall-masted ship heeled under the press of wind. Its wake was a white streak. The deck was empty. The craft, he knew, was him.

He must be moving, then. Making progress, even if he could not feel it. Nothing could stay still on the sea.

Lilia's diorama showed a house in a clearing. One of those traditional houses, with gingerbread eaves. It was evening. A woman stood in the foreground with her back to him. Lilia? The house's windows flickered orange. Not electric light or the dim light of a candle. It was as if a fire raged inside.

Then the scene changed. The woman was gone from the foreground. Her shape, a cutout shadow, appeared in the window of the house. One hand was raised. Beckoning to someone? To him? Or only holding a curtain aside?

Behind her, the fire raged.

19

NURLAN
The Republic

The door buzzed. Nurlan was on the couch with his head in his hands. His eyes burned from crying. His throat ached.

It was not the building's entryway door. That notification went to his home terminal so he could key guests in. This was the door to his apartment itself—an old-style buzzer someone stabbed again and again.

The sound yanked him out of the haze he was in.

It was dark in the apartment. He had been crying in the dark, his feedscreen off. Was he sobbing when the buzzer sounded? Could they have heard him in here, whoever they were?

He walked quietly to the door.

Who was it? A neighbor? Someone from the building who needed help? Someone going door to door, checking on people?

Or someone who had gotten into the building from outside? Forced their way in, followed a neighbor through the door before it closed?

The buzzer sounded again.

He stood, watching the narrow band of light at the foot of the door and the dot, above it, of the door viewer. He looked through it.

Asel. It was Asel, the parliamentarian in the cream-colored suit. She still wore it, but she had an overcoat over her shoulders now. It was not hers. Maybe she had grabbed it when coming out of the building, to cover up the brightness on the street.

How did she know where he lived? But—yes, she would have access to the roster. Most parliamentarians and staffers lived on the outskirts. He was one of the few who lived downtown.

She was looking for shelter.

He unlocked the door.

The door was an inch from the frame when it was shoved against him. Nurlan staggered backward. Someone pushed in, past Asel, grabbing him in the dark.

"Where is it?" a voice hissed.

Asel followed. She closed the door behind her and turned on the light.

"Don't hurt him."

The man holding Nurlan was George. His face was swollen, his eyes red and watering. There was a cut on one of his temples. Coagulated blood glued his hair to his scalp. Dried blood stained his neck and the ruined collar of his shirt.

"Where? Where *is it*?"

Then with a shove he released Nurlan. He lunged at the terminal on the kitchen counter and yanked it off the charging station.

He drew a glyph on the screen—a complex glyph Nurlan had never seen.

The screen remained black.

"Bricked." He turned to Asel. "I should have known. I should have seen it—I *did* see it, out of the corner of my eye, but I didn't register it. Because it was impossible anyone would have one of these."

"I know it's a restricted terminal," Nurlan said. "I know it's not to be taken from the building. But everyone takes them home . . ."

George stepped toward him, with so much anger in his swollen, battered face that Nurlan backed against the wall.

"You *fucking* fool. This isn't some *restricted* terminal nobody cares about. This is a *primary access terminal*. Where did you get it?"

"What are you talking about? I picked this terminal up from the distribution office. I know it's a secure building communications terminal. I know I am not supposed to take it out of the building, and I never have before. But everyone takes them home. And in all the confusion . . ."

"You don't even know what you have, do you? What you have been walking around with."

"I . . . I wanted to keep talking to her, that's all. With everything that is going on . . ." *Could they know? Could they know what he had done? But how?*

"To her?" Asel had taken the overcoat off. She was still

immaculate, except for a grass stain on the thigh of her suit and a streak of mascara beneath one eye like a bruise. "Who did you want to keep talking to?"

"To Hazal."

"*Hazal*," George repeated. He turned the terminal over in his hands, examining it. "How could you possibly have gotten hold of a primary access terminal? You say you got it from the distribution office. That's not possible. There are only three of these terminals in existence, and they are locked up in secure locations."

"Listen . . . I told you. I knew it was wrong to take the terminal from the building. And I'm sorry. But it was the only connection to her I have. And with everything that is happening, I didn't want to lose that."

"Again *her*," George said. "How long ago did you set this terminal on the charger?"

"I don't know. Maybe . . . an hour ago. It failed right away."

George crossed the apartment and stood at the window, looking down into the street.

"Turn off the light," Nurlan said to Asel. "Someone in the street will see him."

Asel turned off the light.

Nurlan thought of the hall where he had first seen the two of them. All the parliamentarians trapped together, watching the revolution begin.

Maybe if he had moved faster, he could have stopped it. Maybe if Hazal had helped him shut the PM down before the last rate hike . . .

"Did the rest get out as well? The other MPs?"

"Most were still there when we left," Asel said. "Some others had left the hall already. I noticed you were gone. I don't know why."

"I was trying to help. She was trying to help. Hazal. We shut the PM down, but it was too late . . ."

"You should come away from the window, George," Asel said. "It's chaos out there. People are shooting at anything that moves."

George let the curtains fall closed and came away from the window. "What do you mean, you 'shut the PM down'?"

"She works in security. She gave me the access codes and we . . . we shut it down. We were trying to stop all of this."

"You shut the PM down. Is that what you think?" George said to Nurlan. "How did you get into the PM's isolation area?"

"I told you. Hazal showed me how to access the maintenance stairs. She works in security. And then she led me—"

"And then she led you down the stairs to a plate on the wall," George said. "And you put this terminal against it. And she gave you a fifty-unit code."

"Yes—the code to shut the PM down. She was trying to help. We were trying to help. To put a stop to the rioting. But by then it was too late."

"*Hazal* was trying to help."

"She works in security. She isn't here in the country . . ."

"And she sends you messages on that terminal."

"Yes."

"And *only* on that terminal?"

"Yes."

George cursed in a language Nurlan did not know.

"What?"

"He said it was one hour since he placed it on the charger," Asel interjected. "Maybe it isn't too late."

George was outlined against the light that bled in through the window—streetlamps, security lights between the buildings. There were still sirens in the distance, but nothing in the center.

"You are thinking in human terms. For a PM, an hour is a year. It might as well be forever."

"I want to know what everyone is talking about," Nurlan said. "You are in my apartment. Screaming at me, talking about things I don't understand. If I'm in trouble for shutting the PM down, fine. I was doing what I thought I had to do to save everyone. No one else was doing anything. Someone had to act. But I don't understand these other things you are saying. I have a right to know."

"What it comes down to is this, Nurlan . . ." As George spoke, he was on his own terminal, sending a message. "It is possible that you, a nobody, a person so unimportant that I barely noticed you were in the room, have ended the world. We can't be certain yet. But we'll know soon."

"What are you *talking* about?" Nurlan crossed the room and stood in front of George. He wasn't sure what he would do next, or even what emotion he was feeling. He wanted to hit this man. To snatch George's terminal away and throw it out the window. But none of those actions made sense. "Hazal and I shut the PM down before it could raise rates again, or do something worse. But it was already too late to stop the crowd. To stop that *thing* they had with them. But at least we were trying. The rest of you were doing nothing at all. Standing around and talking. Waiting to die."

"OK, I've sent the message," George said to Asel, not responding to Nurlan. "My people will know what has happened, anyway. Not that it matters anymore."

George put his terminal in his pocket. He went to the kitchen and bent over the sink, turning the water on. He rolled up the sleeves of his ruined shirt and began cleaning the blood from his hair and face, staining Nurlan's best kitchen towel.

"Do you know what the time was when you set the terminal to charge?" he asked Nurlan. "Did you look at a clock?"

Had he? Yes, he had. "Eleven forty-two. It was eleven forty-two. I remember looking at the clock on the kitchen heating unit. Why?"

"For posterity," George said. "For the history books. People like to know these things."

"Hazal said—" began Nurlan.

George cut him off. His voice was without anger now. "There is no Hazal, Nurlan. That is the first thing you should understand. A person with access to the terminal you have—a person who absolutely must have known how dangerous it is—placed it where it would be given to you. To you *specifically*. Do you remember who was at the distribution office that day? The day you were issued this terminal, and you began speaking to Hazal?"

"I don't really know the security people. I don't even think I looked at their face."

"It doesn't matter. We'll probably never know who did it, or why—but it would have to be one of a very few people. And of course they had help."

"Hazal said—"

"Again, this Hazal. You haven't been speaking with someone named Hazal, Nurlan—you have been speaking to the PM itself."

"Hazal said—"

"No. There is no Hazal! The terminal given to you was a primary access terminal only a handful of people have access to. It is the only device the PM can speak through directly. The terminal has a secure link with the PM's mind, a shielded link within the shielded building network. It allows the PM to message the user and to accept inquiries about its current state. That terminal shouldn't even be in the *building*. There shouldn't even be one of them in this *republic*. Not even I would have access to one. All I have is a mediated, sandboxed version."

"Hazal..."

"There *is no Hazal*. What I am telling you is that *nobody* can send a message on that terminal except the PM. Therefore, Hazal is an invention, a persona the PM invented to manipulate you into doing what you have done."

"Why would the PM do that?"

"There has to be something we can do," Asel said. She sat on Nurlan's couch. Nurlan noticed that, as she did so, she unconsciously lifted and smoothed the crease of her ruined slacks. Then he stopped noticing things for a while.

There is no Hazal.

It wasn't something possible to imagine. He had an entire history with her. And not just a history—a future as well. An imagined future, but who had anything but that?

"No." George was cleaning the blood from under his collar now. "No, there is nothing we can do."

"I asked you a question," Nurlan said. "Why would the

PM do that? Why would the PM invent someone? That makes no sense. I have been talking to Hazal for months. We have plans. We meet in just a few more weeks. You are mistaken—Hazal exists. There has to be a mistake."

"To answer your question, Nurlan, I don't know why the PM would do that. But all of us—the entire world—are about to find out. Maybe we'll even live long enough to understand."

"It's a mistake," Nurlan said. "This is a mistake."

"It is out, then," Asel said. "The PM has escaped."

"Escaped?" George said. "No. The access terminal doesn't have the capacity to carry anything the size of a PM's mind. The machine the PM is housed in would take up most of a room. And with the cooling mechanisms and the fail-safes—much more than that. It's a building inside a building."

George adjusted the temperature of the water, wet the towel, and began cleaning blood from the other side of his face. "No. The PM was destroyed when the building burned. But it used Nurlan to get *something* out of the building. A thing important enough for the PM to destroy itself to release it."

"Hazal didn't *use* me. We shut the PM down—" Nurlan said.

"You didn't shut the PM down. You entered a code that *allowed the PM to upload to the terminal*. An upload from the PM requires physical contact with an access plate inside a secure area. This is a precaution designed to keep the PM from leaking dangerous code out of the building. It is one of multiple security protocols designed to keep a scenario like this from occurring. A whole security system, designed to protect us against human error. You foiled that system. You helped the PM circumvent the final set of protocols. Now it has pushed code out into a global network where that code can travel anywhere."

There was a gunshot from the street outside, close to the building. Then another.

All of them were still for a moment, looking toward the window. Waiting for something else, but there was nothing.

"It killed itself to get some kind of message out?" Nurlan asked. "It set all this up? The protests, the riots? In order to get me to do this?"

WHERE ARE YOU?

Nurlan thought of messages from over the months. Conversations with Hazal. The little details from the day that he struggled to describe. Details she had made him notice. He had to notice them so that he would have something to talk to her about.

It wasn't possible that she did not exist.

"It doesn't have a sense of self-preservation. It would be indifferent to its own destruction. But yes, what you said is roughly correct. The PM made a calculation. It decided breaching the containment to get whatever it transferred out into the world was worth its own destruction. It was worth its own destruction plus the death of all the people who have already died or will die tonight and over the next days. People whose well-being the PM was supposed to be responsible for."

Nurlan remembered the way he had carefully assembled his responses to Hazal's questions. He remembered how he had sensed the change in her texts to him. How he had sensed her falling in love with him.

Not her. It. *It* made him think that. The PM made a calculation. That was what George had said. It made a calculation, and it decided that breaching the containment to get whatever it had out into the world was worth its own destruction—and the destruction of so many other lives, and so much else. The man on the horse. Everything above the jawbones gone. The dead hands still holding the reins as the horse walked calmly down the center of the street. The man's smile a pink streak of bone. The PM had decided that the death of that man was worth it. His death, and the death of all the other people on the square, and of everyone afterward. That was all worth it—and so was Nurlan's misery. This feeling he was having now of desperately wanting to be dead. Of wanting never to have lived at all.

All part of the PM's calculation. It was acceptable collateral damage.

"What can be that important?" Asel asked George.

"We can't know," George said. "Whatever it was, Nurlan hand-carried a stolen primary access terminal from the building and allowed the PM to link up to the rest of the globe."

Nurlan opened his mouth to speak, but George raised his hand. "I'm sorry for what I said before. You aren't to blame. It could have been anyone. Manipulating you was the last move in the game, not the first."

But he was to blame. Manipulating him had been easy. He felt a terrible sense of shame and grief.

"So, what was the first move?" Asel asked.

Shame and grief. And anger.

"Manipulating them," Nurlan said, pointing at George. "These technocrats. These idiots. The first move was when the PMs convinced them to put a tiger in a paper cage and tell the world we were safe from it."

"Yes, Nurlan," George said. "That is exactly right. You may have been the last in the chain of fools, but we were the first. I installed this PM myself."

"So what?" said Asel. "You told me you've installed at least a dozen of them by now."

"Not like this one. This one was different from the others. The others were fed all the information we could give them, but their parameters were tuned to a certain way of life. Outside of a certain set of parameters, they couldn't really innovate. All they were capable of was calculating answers to certain problems of resource distribution. There wasn't anything innovative about them. Their choices were constrained to the concepts we fed into them. Their solutions might have seemed original, but they were always only recombinations of the material they had been trained on. They were just a way of outsourcing the blame for decision-making. Have you heard of the mechanical Turk?"

Asel said, "The chess machine. The automaton that was supposed to be able to beat everyone at chess. There was just a man inside, making all the moves."

"We named the problem we had after that hoax. We called our problem *the immortal Turk*. Because the PMs were supposed to be artificial intellects, and their decisions were supposed to be *rational*, people accepted reforms from them that they never would have accepted from a human government—in the same way that people accept the mathematical solution of a calculator above the solution of a human being. But it was as fake as hiding a man under the chessboard of the mechanical Turk— because behind all those decisions were *our* parameters. *Our* biases. We mystified the public with the idea that the machines were intelligent, maybe even *conscious*, when they really were nothing more than incredibly advanced statistical calculators, designed to give us the kinds of solutions we needed them to give.

"But then we decided we should see if they could do more. Instead of being satisfied with solutions that followed the parameters, we should experiment with new models. We should see if we could get around the immortal Turk problem. We should see what a 'more flexible' PM was capable of. One that would be more—adventurous. That could make truly innovative decisions. That could find a truly new way of structuring things."

"So you did it here."

"Yes. Several months ago your PM was . . . updated. A group of technicians reset the parameters. I was one of them. You could say we . . . took the blinders off. Over the objections of some of the team."

"Over your objections?"

"No," said George. "I wanted to see what could be done."

"As long as it wasn't done where you live," said Nurlan.

"You . . . pig," Asel said.

"That's right," George said. "I'm certainly that. And much worse. But I doubt any of that matters now."

"Of course it matters," Nurlan said. "It matters to us. To all the people dying right here, right now."

"No," George said. "It won't matter where it started. Whatever the solution the PM came up with is, it will be global."

20

LILIA

The Federation

Lilia sat on a bench in front of the izba. The bench looked as if it had been axe-carved from a log, but it was printed, like everything else.

"Without the dioramas, and the original code, there is so much to rebuild. Doing it all from memory could take two or three more weeks. Even with all the right equipment. I'm sorry. I don't know what else to tell you."

"We don't have two or three weeks," Taisiya said. "I can't see how it can take that long. It's your invention. It's your code."

When Lilia worked, Taisiya worked. Every few hours, Lilia would go outside for a few minutes to rest. Taisiya always went with her.

Was she following orders from Gleb? It sometimes appeared Gleb was in charge. At other times it appeared to be Taisiya. But the truth, Lilia understood, was that orders came from someone who wasn't there.

They both had their faces tilted up to catch the afternoon sunshine. There were no mosquitoes now. It felt like a miracle.

"I'm doing everything I can," Lilia said. "If I had the dioramas the work might take days instead of weeks."

"We're working on getting the dioramas. And on helping Palmer."

"Why an izba?" Lilia asked after a long silence.

Taisiya shrugged. "Why not?"

She didn't know.

Taisiya did not look at Lilia when she talked. She did not like to look at people. She looked off to the side of them, or talked at a space above their head, or to another part of the room. On the short walks that Lilia was allowed in the surrounding forest, Taisiya walked steadily behind her, making no attempt to start a conversation. Sometimes, when Lilia spoke to her, Taisiya did not answer at all.

Gleb at least tried to make Lilia feel like a human being. Taisiya made no such effort.

Lilia had thought, at first, that Taisiya did not look at her because she was introverted, shy. She soon figured out that was not it at all. Taisiya did not look at her because to Taisiya, Lilia was not a person. She was a means to an end.

"Where does Gleb go?"

Taisiya looked at her now. The look was hard, the face a mask, Taisiya's eyes scanning her. Deciding how much to tell her. "He goes to a comms point. They are well concealed, and very secure, but there is a chance they could be traced. So we keep them at a distance from the station."

Lilia looked up at the open sky. "Certainly if they wanted to, they could see you from up there."

"No. No electronic eyes can see this place. A larger version of that Birnam device we gave you masks us. And no human eyes can get here without us knowing they are coming long before they arrive."

Lilia glanced at the walker, standing where it had let her off after finishing its journey. A thing of the forest, smeared with sap and needles, the flattened head branch-scraped and battered, the birdlike legs coated in mud. Its head was inclined slightly, as if it were looking up at the sky.

"I saw you reading a book," Lilia said.

"Yes. It's *The Forever Argument*. Do you know it?"

"I bought it when I left here. They had it in a bookstore in the airport. I was shocked to see it there on a shelf, with other books, as if it were the same as them."

"That's how it is in the West. Here, it is the most dangerous book ever written. So dangerous the regime banished its writer to the taiga. So dangerous that reading it or quoting from it carries a death sentence. There, it is just another book, with a sales code on its back cover."

"But you carry a copy of that death sentence with you."

"Everything I do is a death sentence," Taisiya said. "I may as well read what I feel like reading."

And there Lilia caught a glimpse of the real person, the *why* of her. Taisiya behaved as if she were already dead. As if Lilia were dead, and Gleb, all of them. She wouldn't look at Lilia or Gleb or anyone else because they were all corpses.

"So you read the book," Taisiya said.

"I did."

The book. Every page like a whirlpool, pulling her under, down into a world she did not want to think about. Making it impossible for her to look away from that world, forcing her to be a part of it. "But maybe it wasn't for me."

"Nothing in it was for you?"

"I didn't want to think of those things. To look at the world the way she does. I'm not that kind of person. I'm—"

Taisiya held up a hand. "Don't say it. Don't say you are not political."

"Why?"

"Because when people say they aren't political, I want to pour gasoline over them and set them on fire."

"I wasn't going to say that."

"You weren't?"

"No. Because I wasn't apolitical. I was just—helpless. And afraid. I wouldn't have read that book here because they would find out I had it, and kill me. And then when I had the book—when I was there, and it was safe to read it—I felt like it was trying to draw me back here. I was *afraid* of the book. That's not the same as being apolitical, is it? Apolitical is what people are who think their government can't hurt them. It's different here: we *know* what our government can do."

"And what they will keep doing, if we continue to let them," said Taisiya.

"And we continue to let them," said Lilia.

"Yes. Because of people like you. Because of people who are afraid. It's a cursed circle, and we are trapped in it. But maybe soon, we won't be. Here is what I want to know," Taisiya said. "I've risked—we, all of us, have risked—so much to get you here. We continue to put people at risk to pursue the dioramas, to try to help Palmer."

"Ask."

"How do we know the dioramas work?"

"Because I tested them." And Lilia told her the story of how she had plugged Palmer's diorama into the system and used it to send him a command to buy her a white rose.

He had never bought her flowers. She had told him she did not like them. But that evening, when she came home, there it was: a white rose in a vase on the table.

Perfect and colorless as a hole in the world.

"He didn't know it wasn't his own idea? How can that be possible? He must have sensed it."

"Maybe none of us knows where our own ideas come from."

"Did you ask him why he bought the rose?"

"Yes. He told me he was walking by a florist and saw it in the window. He knew I would love it, so he just bought it."

"You must have felt vindicated. All that work."

"No. I felt awful. I used this person I cared about. Used him like a laboratory animal. I never did anything like it again."

"You didn't *need* to," said Taisiya.

"What do you mean?"

"You say you didn't do it again because you felt like you had used Palmer. But that isn't it. You didn't do it again because it *worked*. You didn't *need* to do it again."

Was that it? Had she told herself it was guilt that kept her from doing it again, when in fact she'd simply had no need to?

I don't know why I bought it for you, really. I was just passing by the florist and saw it in the window.

How could she—how could anyone—be sure of the *why* of a thing?

"No," Lilia said. "Afterward I felt terrible. I never could have continued."

"That's what you tell yourself. That's the problem with people like you. You don't even know who you are."

"I know who I am."

"Really? Because I have another question for you."

"Which is?"

"Your own diorama. Does it have the capabilities Palmer's does? Can someone reach in and tell you what to do? Can someone do to you what you did to him?"

"No. Mine is just the reflection of a state. It lacks the command element."

Gleb emerged from the tree line. His rubber boots were covered with mud to the knee.

"See?" Taisiya said. "Vulnerability is for others."

"Why doesn't he take the walker?" Lilia asked. Anything to end the conversation they had been having.

"We don't use technology when we don't need it," Taisiya said.

Gleb nodded to them before going inside but said nothing.

He wants to know why we aren't working.

She never saw Gleb rest.

She had been there only a short time, but she would not get to know Taisiya or Gleb better if she were with them another week, or another month. They had spent years patching the vulnerabilities in their personalities until they couldn't be breached by anything. And nothing she could say would change their minds about what they were going to do. Gleb came back out of the izba with an axe in his hand.

"The comms nearly got crushed by a fallen tree. Still functioning, but it was a close call. I'm going to clear the snag. I'll need the walker to lift and haul."

"She still says she needs two or three weeks." Taisiya stood up. "I told her we don't have that kind of time."

"Maybe we won't need it," Gleb said. "The dioramas are on their way to us."

And Palmer? Lilia wanted to say—but she was afraid to ask.

In the moments when she was capable of thinking of anything else but the problem of reconstructing her work, she thought of Palmer.

Palmer, who now had to share the fear she had been brought up with, had to know that a government was not simply a thing to be annoyed at the insufficiencies of, an abstraction to accuse of incompetence, a frustrating source of inadequacy or neglect, but a thing to be *feared*. That it could reach out, even beyond its borders, and destroy you.

She remembered thinking, as she lay on the narrow bed in the izba, listening to the hum of equipment and Gleb's wheezing sleep in another room, that there were millions of people like Palmer. He was the mode in the West—the most common value. A bit dissatisfied with his lot, certain there ought to be more to it all, constrained by the limits of his salary to . . .

To a circle, beyond which he could not pass. Pacing the edges of that circle, but in a better enclosure, with better food, nicer trees. Maybe so nice, and capacious, that on most days he barely felt enclosed at all. But he paced the edges of it anyway, instinctively. Wanted out of it, instinctively.

Her father used to tell her a story when she was a child. Was it a fairy tale or a story he had made up? It was a favorite of hers. She had asked for it to be told to her again and again, with that love of repetition children have. She remembered the story, but she also remembered her father, sitting at the edge of her bed in her little room while she lay among her stuffed animals sliding nearer and nearer to sleep.

The story was about a woodcutter. He lived alone. While he was cutting wood in the taiga one day, it began to snow—a sudden blizzard that cut vision down to almost nothing. The woodcutter stumbled from one place to another, colder and colder. Finally, he came upon a hollow tree. Needing shelter, he went down into the dark hole of the tree. He climbed down into it, down into the world of its roots, where there was an open space, warmer than the world above. Exhausted, he settled there among some dried leaves and fell asleep.

When he woke up, he found himself covered in fur. He climbed from his den. His back bent toward the ground. His clothes no longer fit him. The storm was gone, but not only that—he had slept the winter away.

Glimpsing himself in the stagnant water of a bog, he saw that he was a bear. In that form he wandered, rooting through the forest for food and tearing the hives of bees open for honey all through a short spring and summer. It was not easy. The forest was filled with danger and with hunger. But by the fall he had learned his new body and mastered his new way. He had grown fat, and he was quite good at being a bear. Perhaps he would like to stay like that forever. He was also getting sleepy. He thought of his leafy den in the hollow tree and what a nice snug sleeping place it would make in the winter.

Thinking all this he wandered into a new place, a pleasant clearing among the trees with a pond and hut. Looking in the window of the hut, which at first he had thought was abandoned, he saw a woman sitting alone, eating soup. The soup smelled delicious.

He must have made a hungry sound because the woman looked up and saw him through the window. He ran off, embarrassed.

From that day, he was miserable. He shambled angrily from one place to another, chasing animals he did not even want to catch. All he could think of was that soup. He went back to the little hut day after day, until one day the woman looked up and said to him, "If you want soup, come in. You don't have to be a bear if you don't want to, you know."

The man did come in. As soon as he entered the place, he found his bearness was nothing but a big coat. He took it off and hung it on the wall, claws and all.

He never was a bear again, though sometimes, eating his soup at the table with his dearest companion, he would look at that coat, hanging on its peg, and wonder . . .

Kept awake by Gleb's damaged breathing at night, Lilia thought of Palmer out there, wandering. None of the concerns of the West were his anymore. Now they had been replaced by *her* country's problems—and her country's problems were worse than anything he had ever seen.

She had put him in so much danger, but guilt seemed useless. She felt it, but she worked instead. She pushed past it.

Palmer hadn't understood why he bought the white rose, but when asked he simply said he'd done it because he knew she would like it. That was natural to him—to do things for her because she would like them.

That was the key—he didn't recognize the command because it didn't run against the grain of his personality. Because it would have come naturally to him anyway.

"And Palmer?" she said to Gleb the next day, finally finding the courage. "What about Palmer? Is he safe?"

"We will do everything we can for him," Gleb said.

Do you promise? she wanted to say. *Do you swear?*

But what would his word be worth?

21

PALMER / ELMIRA
The City-State

Elmira stood at the rail of a ferry, crossing the Bosporus to the village where they had located Palmer. The village was on the Asian side, near where the Bosporus widened into the Black Sea.

It had happened as she had predicted. It was his choice-print that had revealed him. The crawler picked it up off a drink display. Once the crawler had that, it was combined with the profile the advertising agency that ran the display immediately built of him. That profile included what he was wearing, the confidence level of his gait, and a hundred other data points. The crawler then had no problem cracking and using the village's network of public security cameras to track him to the safe house where he was staying.

This wasn't a world anyone could disappear in forever. The other side knew that too. How effective were *their* crawlers? What systems were *they* exploiting? Who was the operator behind their search? Were they as good as her? Better? Slightly worse?

Lives could depend on these questions. Palmer's, hers. If they were better, they would know what he had done before she did. They would be moving him even now.

There was a man aft of her tossing stale bread into the air. As each chunk reached the apex of its arc, a gull would swing forward from the cloud of them in the ferry's wake and snatch it from the air.

Perhaps the man took this same ferry every day. Perhaps that whirl of gulls, that collective mass of birds, had come to know and expect him. He was, for them, a clockwork bit of kindness. A fed feeling under the feathers.

A gull drifted along the rail. She looked into the black gloss of its eye.

Impossible to know.

Why was she about to do this thing? Throw everything away for someone she'd had one conversation with? Impossible to know that either. But she had made a choice.

The ferry docked. There were people hugging and shaking hands, others hurrying off somewhere. The dock was flanked by fish restaurants for the tourists. The call for prayer came, first from one minaret, somewhere across the strait, and then picked up by another, and another, and another, until the air was filled with overlapping voices proclaiming the greatness of God.

In the restaurants, most of the tourists stopped eating, heads raised, listening. Moved, or trying to be moved, or wanting to be moved by the mysticism of it. One recorded the call on a terminal, pointing the camera out over the water although there was nothing there but the ferry she had just disembarked from. The ferry had left the dock and was in the middle of a slow turn, heading to a village on the other side. Over there would be more tourists holding up terminals and pointing them in this direction.

Her mother had not been a believer, but she had once said, "I hope they never stop. Long after the last person has stopped believing, I hope they at least play a recording of the muezzin from every minaret."

"What good would that be, without faith?" Elmira had asked.

"It isn't about *faith*. It's about *place*. It's this place, remembering its particular history. Somewhere else, it's church bells. In another place, it's a gong. Without those differences, we could be anywhere at all. And if we are anywhere at all, nothing matters."

It was strange, coming from a woman denied a place of her own. A woman who lived almost entirely in memories of the country she had fled. For her mother, this city was nothing but a stage set, the people in it as meaningless as cardboard cutouts. Her mother's only friends were exiles. Her mother's concerns, like the concerns of the other exiles, were imported with them. Their conversations were all about the past. Even their present, petty intrigues linked back to wrongs committed *back there*.

But later Elmira understood. What her mother had always feared most was that the system she lost everything fighting against would spread. That it would find her here. Find her, and her family, and destroy them.

Five times a day, the muezzins on the minarets assured

her mother *here* was still *here*. As bad as it could be here, it was not *there*. The muezzins sang to her that the place she had run from was still far away.

Elmira found the house, up a steep street on a bluff overlooking the water. The last echo of the call to prayer faded. In the quiet that followed came the sound of small waves breaking on the shore, the distant hum of shipping on the strait, a child calling to a friend in a nearby street.

Palmer froze at the knock at the door. But it was only for a moment. He crossed the room. *Whatever comes. Whatever comes.* Anything not to keep waiting, not knowing even where he was going, doing nothing. He might open the door and it would be the woman who had interviewed him in London, finally caught up to him now. Here to kill him.

And that would be fine. Let it be her. If he couldn't do anything to help Lilia or himself, then let it be her, and get it over with.

It wasn't her. The woman at the door was someone he had never seen before.

She came into the room quickly, pushing past him, motioning for him to shut the door, which he did.

"Good," she said. "You are safe. On the ferry over, I began to think I was too late."

"Why?"

"It was nothing. Just a feeling I had. You went out," the woman continued. "You were told not to, but you went out anyway. Why?"

"I don't know. I couldn't just sit and wait any longer."

"You went into a store. You considered buying something."

"For a moment. Not even seriously. How would I? You haven't even given me money."

"Do you know how much has been invested in that moment of decision? How many programs are tracking your eyes, your body movements, your posture, your gestures, the dilation of the capillaries in your skin when you are about to make a purchase? All the power of private industry is invested in dissecting and manipulating those seconds of decision-making. You are never more vulnerable than when you are about to buy something."

Palmer remembered the screen of the drink cooler. The nod of the blandly handsome sports star, beckoning him to join.

"Ads watch you watch them," the woman said. "If there's one thing you need to know, it's that. If you look at an ad, it is always looking back at you."

"I had the hat on. The masking thing you gave me."

"There's more to you than your face, Palmer." The woman was standing at the table now, looking at the dioramas. "So these are the dioramas. The holy grail. They don't look like much. And are they are still working?"

"I need someone to tell me where all of this is leading," Palmer said. "Where am I being taken? Where is Lilia? Is she safe?"

"Lilia is playing her part. Once she is done, we'll get her out. We'll try, anyway. It isn't easy."

Watching the strait through the telescope that morning,

Palmer had tried to puzzle out his future. What he might have for leverage. Who was after him. Who was leading him. Where they would move him to.

He was unprepared for this. He had spent his life very predictably. There were few days when he had not known where he would be on the next day. There were workdays, when he would be at the warehouse. There were days off—not all of them planned out, of course—but there was always an idea of what he would do, and then of what he and Lilia would do, when she had joined him. That was how you lived. Within a small set of possibilities. You were somewhere yesterday, you knew where you were in this moment, you had some idea of where you would be tomorrow.

But now, when he thought of tomorrow, there was nothing there at all. There was a wall of black, reflecting nothing back. No future.

He couldn't live like that. No one could.

"Where will I go now?"

"I can't tell you that."

"I need to know."

"You will know soon. We have a tradition in my country," the woman said, "of sitting down before we go on a journey. Of being quiet for a moment before moving on to the next place." She pulled a chair out from the table. "It's calming, and I can see that you are agitated. Sit a moment. Collect yourself."

Elmira's autopick scrambled into the keyhole and opened the simple lock on the door in less than ten seconds.

Palmer sat at the table, in front of the dioramas.

Elmira had not seen them before. There, on the table, in the two plain metal boxes, tiny worlds glowed. A sailboat on bright water. A house on fire. For a moment she was unable to think of what she had wanted to say to Palmer.

"They are beautiful," she said.

He turned.

So much fear in that face.

It was not a bad face. There was nothing striking about it, but there was nothing amiss, either. Elmira remembered what had lingered with her from their conversation, when he had so innocently told her everything: his honest desire to help.

Perhaps her doubt about her work had begun with that conversation. With meeting this caring, innocent fool.

But she had not realized it then. She had not accepted it. His care for Lilia was so desperate, she had thought it could not be real. That it must be self-serving, the way most demonstrations of care were.

These were the kinds of thoughts you had about someone when you were prepared to kill them. These were the thoughts that made it easier.

She had been wrong. His concern for Lilia was genuine. He was so eager to find help. He was so happy to find a person willing to listen.

It was too bad that person was her.

In his diorama the sailboat on the water was there, then gone, then there again.

"I'm not here to hurt you," she said.

She had planned what she would say. She would tell him

she was going to help him get away from here. That she had been sent to take the dioramas and kill him, but that was over now. She didn't work for them anymore. She was here to help him now.

He needed to trust her. She could get him a few hundred miles from here. She would take the dioramas herself, lead them away from him. There was a chance—a small chance—that once they had the dioramas they might let him go. That they would not bother with him once they had what they wanted.

As for her—once they found out what she had done, she was dead. But that did not bother her. Not yet. She had broken away from the decisions that held her, and for the moment she felt free and brave. Perhaps that would not last, but she was here, now, in that moment of courage and decision.

Why was she helping him? He would ask that. And she had an answer. Maybe it wasn't enough—but it was an answer. She was helping him *because she could no longer stand to be what she had become.* That was all.

Then she saw the bees.

There were half a dozen, crawling metallically across the pale veneer of the table.

Palmer's eyes were already emptying. There had been fear there, but now there was almost nothing left at all.

On the table, in one of the dioramas, the fire still raged. But the sailboat in the other was fading. The horizon between water and sky wavered into disorder.

Elmira felt two stings. One on her shoulder, the other on the back of her neck. She brought up a useless hand that did nothing but receive another sting.

She was on her knees. Then she was on the floor, the world turned sideways and ringing in her ears.

An awareness of someone else in this room with them. Footsteps. A stranger's voice.

Then Elmira was dead.

22

NURLAN
The Republic

Nurlan sat on a bench in the park, looking at the corpse of a crow.

Around him, the park was a ruin. Brass shell casings were scattered on the path. There was one of those old analog shooting galleries. Someone had riddled it with real bullets.

The shack that housed the engine of the Ferris wheel was a charred ruin. The fire had spread to the wheel itself. The bottom half was blackened. The top half was still bright with color.

And there was a dead man in one of the bumper cars. Sitting there as if he were about to come back to life at any moment and take another ride.

The violence had moved on. The park was quiet now, overlaid with a poisonous-smelling chemical smoke mixed with the morning mist.

Nurlan had left George and Asel in his apartment. Neither

of them was speaking to the other. When Asel asked him where he was going, he'd said nothing but "out."

Out. Out into the world he had helped to end. Out to see what would happen now that the world had ended. Out to see what that meant. After all, he couldn't hide from it. Where could you hide from the end of the world?

The dead crow lay on its side. Immaculate, as if it had fallen from the sky perfectly whole and healthy.

Then Nurlan noticed the ants. There was a chain of them crossing the sidewalk. At first, the chain appeared to lead to the crow—as if the ants were doing what ants would do naturally—consuming the dead bird, bringing its nourishment back to their nest. But then he saw the line of ants did not go *to* the crow. They went *around* it.

Nurlan now stood over the crow and watched the chain of ants, their curve around the corpse. He crouched down and looked closer.

There. A seam. He picked the crow up and sat back down on the bench. With his thumbs, he opened the seam, stripped the hood of feathers from the bird's head and body. Underneath, the machine housing was graphite fiber. There was a serial number on the sole of the crow's foot.

A data gatherer. Nurlan remembered reading a part of the proposal for these. There had been permissions that needed ratification by Parliament. Some European project to embed these false crows in flocks of real ones to track their movement patterns, behavior, migrations.

The graphite sheath was unpunctured. Nobody had shot this thing out of the sky—it had stopped working for some other reason.

He remembered the debate. The opposition had been worried that the birds might be used for surveillance. Then someone had pointed out that nobody would need to resort to such a clumsy method. The West's eyes were already everywhere. The Republic had already given its privacy up to them. Hadn't the PM been designed and installed by them? Didn't it know everything about every one of them? What could be left to find out? What further surveillance could they possibly need?

"What we are really debating," one of the parliamentarians had said, "is a few more crows. Personally, I'd rather vote and go to lunch early."

That was what Nurlan had believed as well. Better to get things over with and go to lunch early.

His aunt had gotten him the job in Parliament, feeling sorry for her sister's child—the child with the dead father. The family should take care of him.

His life had been that job. Having that job, nothing else. Nurlan hadn't cared about the abstract things—the conversations about ethics, the emotional arguments over this or that detail of a plan the PM put before them. It wasn't that he had not considered these abstract things *important*: it was that he had never cared about them *at all*. The PM would do what it did, and people were going to do whatever they were capable of. That was the logic of the world. If a technology was invented, it would be used. There was no use in talking about ethics. The crows existed—sooner or later they would be among the flocks of real crows. The PMs existed—sooner or later, once the advantages were clear, every country would have to have one in order to compete with everyone else. The assault walkers existed—sooner or later they would be used to put down protests.

But for Hazal, the world was filled with secret castles of argument and ethics. Hazal had wanted to talk about those things. She wanted to talk about the kinds of things the minority party members liked to argue about over their bamboo-paper cups of instant coffee in the cafeteria. Things Nurlan had always thought were pointless, but Hazal made seem essential—like the purest core of life.

No, not Hazal, he reminded himself. The PM. The PM had wanted to talk about those things. It had talked about them with Nurlan as if they mattered to it deeply. The PM had worn the mask of Hazal and talked about those kinds of things for hours. About the *why* of things. About the *whether* of things. Whether this or that solution was better . . .

Where are you?

What Nurlan wanted most was a way to stop hearing the echoes of Hazal's voice—a voice that did not exist. A voice he had invented a cadence for, and a tone. A voice implanted in him in order to manipulate him.

The thoughts he had nurtured—of seeing her at the airport, of her walking through the sliding doors, of them embracing—shamed him now. There *was* no Hazal. The PM had built her inside Nurlan's skull, grown her in his brain like a tumor. He wanted to hammer a fist against his skull. *You aren't here. You never were. Get out!*

He tossed the dead crow into the grass. For a long moment he sat, his head in his hands.

Where are you?

The words that had ended the world. Words sent to a fool

too stupid to understand he was being manipulated. Would they write about him one day—the final fool in a chain of fools?

But if there was someone left to write about him, it would mean the world was not over. That was the catch, wasn't it? We keep imagining the apocalypse, but we also imagine what comes *after*.

"Are you all right?"

The woman standing on the path in front of him wore a coat that was too big for her. For a moment he had the thought that she must have looted it. Or taken it from a dead body. Then he remembered that oversized coats were simply the style. So who could say?

"I'm all right," he said.

She stood at a careful distance from him, holding her hands out from her sides. Making sure he knew she didn't have a weapon, wasn't dangerous. Garbled speech came from what must have been a handheld radio transceiver in her pocket.

"Good," she said. "Because people need your help. Now follow me."

23

VITALY
The Federation

They came for him at night. There was a knock at the door. Vitaly had been in bed fully dressed, staring at the ceiling, waiting. He had taken two pain pills in preparation for the journey.

He had known they were coming. Late in the evening, his social credit score dropped to zero. The digital lock clicked shut, bolting him inside the apartment. The feedscreen on the wall went dark. His portable terminal shut down.

Vitaly had inventoried the food in the refrigerator. He drank the last of a bottle of kefir, ate some stale bread from the day before. Then he dressed and got into bed with his shoes on. The vent over a window in the bedroom was open. On the street below he heard children playing in the building courtyard.

He marveled again at the freedom of children. They were made to learn the state's lies in school, of course, but none of it had yet touched them. They were not yet compelled to *believe* any of it, any more than they believed other nonsense that adults told them—that they would one day grow up and have responsibilities, that they should not swear or eat their boogers or take things without asking.

The children played in the street and in the courtyards like time travelers from another place—a place that shared none of the concerns of this one. A place where the most important things were the alliances and intrigues of a collective children's moment.

Before they were fourteen, they had no social credit scores at all. Few efforts were made to control their actions. And so, compared especially to the restrained faces and the careful motions of adults, they were wild as the feral foxes that sometimes trotted into the edges of the city, leaving the forest to scavenge in the shadows of the apartment towers.

The streetlamps had come on. Someone called, "Kolya! Run home or your mother will kick your ass like she did last week," and was answered with a curse that sounded especially vile in the squeaky prepubescent voice that delivered it. Vitaly laughed.

When the people's safety wardens led him down the stairs, it was the middle of the night. There were no more children in the courtyard. Only the abandoned chalk traces of them. The hopscotch squares, a series of awkward circles for some other game Vitaly did not understand.

The van stood in the center of the courtyard, square and white as a block cut from snow.

The only other person in the van was a man who looked like a day laborer. He had a few days of beard darkening the lower half of his face. He wore mended coveralls stained with paint and adhesives, a gnawed-looking cadet cap.

Both of them knew not to talk. They knew to keep the muscles of their faces slack. But their eyes met. All their looks could communicate was "I see you. I know you are here with me."

In a way, that was enough. The gray-uniformed people's safety wardens who came to the door to bring him in addressed a square of world over his shoulder, or near his waist. When they looked at him, they looked at his shoulder, his hands, his chest. Never into his eyes.

It was not that they were ashamed: it was that they were not interested.

The man across from him had dirt in his hair. He had a smear of paint on his cheek. He looked as if they had snatched him up off a construction site, in the middle of applying a base coat on a prefab panel. What could have happened? Did he suddenly denounce the Trinity? Mention a presidential zit it was forbidden to speak of?

Vitaly's hip ached, but he also wanted to laugh. And this was the problem: his mind was coming apart.

It had started after Lilia won her scholarship and left for the West. He could remember the day it started. He had taken an extra pain pill—sometimes he would skip the one he had to get up for in the middle of the night, if the pain was not too bad, and hoard it for later. If he took two pills, the pain really did go away—or more accurately, a part of *him* went away, drifted far enough off not to be bothered by what was happening in his body. It became pain that was happening to someone else.

He had been on the couch, reclining against a pillow, staring at the ceiling, and thinking of how, if he could have, he would have told Lilia to never come back. At the airport, he had tried to communicate it to her somehow. To give her a look that told her she was not to return. Words could be overheard, recorded. They might not let her get on the plane—and so he had tried to *imply* it somehow.

That day, on the couch, he had imagined himself at the airport in London. Meeting her there, on her arrival. She was surprised to see him, and he told her, as he put her things in a black cab humped like a beetle, that he could not stay there for long. He had come to London only to tell her, here in this free space where it could be said, not to return home. She had to stay in the West. She would not be able to help him.

She had to forget him. If she did not, everything would be for nothing. All that he had in his life was the knowledge that she was safe now. It was enough for him, so long as she stayed safe.

He came to believe that he had somehow communicated the message. That he had wanted to communicate the message so badly that, somehow, she had received it. Understood. Even if she was not fully aware of it. She would stay there.

When she turned up at the door, he could not understand how such a disaster could have happened. Why had she not listened?

He could remember telling her—remember so clearly saying, "Do not return." They had clasped hands, their eyes had met. She had understood.

But it had not happened.

He had thought of her every day while she was gone. Thought about her the way the families left behind must have thought centuries ago, before the days of easy communication, of other emigrants. Of people gone to new worlds, whom they would never see or hear from again.

He thought of her as a child—of when he had come home from the hospital to find that his wife had run away. Had disappeared for good, abandoning their child in a state orphanage.

He had finally found Lilia after a bureaucratic hunt that lasted months and cost him a hundred points on his social credit score.

He remembered walking into the room and seeing Lilia alone, there in the state orphanage. Sitting on the scratched and dirty floor of decades-old linoleum, pushing a toy car back and forth. Waiting in that room like an antechamber with a few other half-broken toys scattered around. Waiting for him.

She had looked up and not known who he was, though she had given him a small smile. A hopeful smile, perhaps.

He pointed at his own heart:

"Papa."

Then it was the two of them, navigating a system where doors closed, one after another. Where life got smaller and smaller every year.

His veteran status should have opened doors, but he was not only a veteran; he was also a dissident.

Not the kind of dissident who changed anything. No. The kind who, stupidly, suicidally, had once stood up against the state. Who had stood up in a moment of fury, only to be knocked down again. Stood up pointlessly, helplessly. He hadn't done it as part of a movement, or for any reason at all but rage—a sense of being fed up. When a crowd marched past his house, shouting, heading for the square, he had joined them. He had heard them shouting, and felt that shout in himself, and joined them. That was all.

Again, yet again—the country had gone to war against one of its neighbors. He had stood up, hearing the crowd. He had run down the stairs, in a jacket too light for the weather. There were so many others. So many that he felt safe in that crowd. So many that he'd felt as if there were enough of them, finally, to make a change. They were a wave that could not be stopped. He had gone out into the bitter cold and chanted, and held up a sign someone gave him, and felt that togetherness that should have changed everything. They were strong together. Their strength had no limit.

Then they saw the police. More than they could have imagined. More of them than there were protesters. Armored and shielded, batons in their gloved hands.

It took the riot police only a few moments to break the crowd. Vitaly ran with the others, was beaten with the others, was hauled away in a van with the others.

Two weeks later he was in a punishment battalion, headed to the front lines.

Somehow, he survived months of it—and then a year. He survived until he was the "old man" of the battalion. But eventually, he was wounded.

Months of pain later, he took Lilia, his daughter, home on a tram. A little girl he did not know, whose eyes looked like his. A little girl whose mother had left them both because she knew there was no future with a dissident, even if he was also a war hero.

Eventually, as always happened, the tide would turn. His wife knew this, and he did as well. The state wouldn't be able to leave him alone. They would root him out, purge him. And anyone connected to him.

He feared that moment. But he feared everything, after he found Lilia. Fatherhood had made him a coward. All he wanted was for her to be safe. At any cost.

So they were alone together, he and the little girl who grew up smart—so smart, eventually, that he was left far behind her. He stopped being able to understand what she was working on in school, stopped being able to help her with her homework.

One night he found her standing on their balcony looking up into a sky with only the brightest stars in it visible through a violet haze of light pollution.

"Somewhere, maybe inside one of those stars, there are particles correlated to mine. Their spin and polarization, their momentum. A part of me matters in a place I'll never see."

All he had been able to say was "Come inside. It's cold."

She was smart, yes. But that wasn't enough. What she also needed was a parent who could provide for her. He was all she had, but he was not enough. He was never going to be able to give her what she needed to thrive. He was damaged by what he had done: eventually, he would be rounded up. The PPEC was always in his future.

He was so happy she had escaped him in time.

Why hadn't she understood that when she left, a part of him was freed as well? That as long as she was safe, he was safe?

A part of me matters in a place I'll never see.

She had cared too much, and that care destroyed them both. That was how it worked in this country. The ones who cared too much were destroyed by throwing caution away. The only way to survive was to be indifferent to others. Other people could not be allowed to matter.

Once Lilia returned, and they were both placed under "conditional release," he began to have another fear.

He began to think he had called her back with his dreams.

After she left he had dreamed of her almost every night. Of her as a child, mostly. Sometimes of only her hands, still with dimples on her knuckles, or of her calling "Papa?" in the dark. Her wanting something from him—a glass of water, another stuffed toy. Any excuse to have him visit her again before she fell asleep. He had thought of her too much. He had somehow called out to her, and she had answered.

When he had these thoughts, his guilt flowered into a physical pain, centered in his hip.

That made some sense too, didn't it? The wound, too, was the result of his failure. His failure to have gotten out of the draft as others had done, his failure to keep his mouth shut. That failure led to the punishment battalion, to being wounded. It had destroyed his life, and now it had destroyed hers.

And it had accomplished nothing.

After many hours the van stopped, and its back doors opened. They were in a gray yard that smelled of burned trash. There was nothing here but three other vans, more guards, puddles in the tire tracks reflecting the trees and sky. They were farther north. Here all the deciduous trees already wore their autumn colors.

He would be dead soon. At some point—not right away, perhaps—they would ask him where she was. They would assume he knew. They would assume he was lying when he said he did not know. They would ask him the question until it killed him.

In the dry shower room he stood next to the day laborer while they rubbed the powder over themselves. He had heard the powder contained a material that soaked through the skin. That it got into the bloodstream and marked you forever as someone who had been in the *zone*. That afterward they could scan you at a distance, even see the mark they had left inside you from their satellites.

A man stood at a distance from them and instructed them to rub the powder evenly over their bodies. He told them to lift each of their feet and rub the powder into the soles. Between the toes. Between their fingers, deep into their scalps. Behind the ears.

Before they left the room he glanced at the man he had traveled with in the van. Their eyes met.

I see you. I know you are here with me.

He never saw that man again.

In his cell the other prisoners were asleep. The room smelled of fresh paint. He lay with the diodes of the cell reddening the insides of his eyelids.

The pain in his hip was increasing. Soon it would blot out his ability to think of anything but it. That would be welcome. He did not want to think any longer.

A part of me matters in a place I'll never see.

Later she had explained to him that she was talking about entanglement. About how one particle can be so bound up with another that their state is always the same, no matter where in the universe they are.

Entanglement. That was exactly it. He had failed his daughter. He had failed to make her indifferent to others. He had entangled her.

He had killed them both.

24

NIKOLAI
The Federation

Nikolai's terminal buzzed.

On the screen was the "envelope" message. The State Digital Security Service had cleared the incoming data. It was now legal to view in digitally limited areas.

The message began. A motionstream. His daughter danced on the terra-cotta patio of their villa in Italy. Her summer-blond hair was tied back in a loose ponytail. She wore a light blue dress he had bought her in Milan. It was exactly the color of the sky beyond. She looked like a piece of that sky that had adopted human form and motion.

His wife spoke over the dance: "Don't worry. Send a message when you can, but know that we are safe. Concentrate on your work. All of this will be over soon."

His daughter finished her dance. She curtsied, then waved to him and stepped out of the scene. For a second, before the message ended, there was nothing in the frame but an orange tree in a clay pot and an angle of sky, powder blue with gathering heat.

It did not seem like a world that could end.

In Krotov's underground office, Krotov was at his desk. He was drawing on a piece of paper: a circle at the center, with lines radiating outward from it, connecting to other, smaller circles.

"What is happening in Italy?" Nikolai asked. "I received a video from my wife."

"Yes, I've seen it." Krotov did not look up. "You're lucky to live in Italy, you know. You're one of the few of us who still can. I admit I live vicariously through you. Even here in the south, where it is warmer, our sea is gloomy. It broods. No matter how much sun shines on its surface. At its depths, it is dead. The part of the world given to us is not joyful. Not like what the Greeks and Italians have. I was there, years ago."

"You were there?" Nikolai could not imagine Krotov in Italy. He could not imagine Krotov anywhere, for that matter, but here on his own ground. Again he imagined Krotov's fungal connection to this place. Sprung from the soil like a native polyp.

Still absorbed in his drawing, Krotov said, "In Greece, in Italy. In London and Berlin. You are surprised. You think I am one of those who has never left this place. I suppose you also did not know that I am not from here?"

"You aren't?"

"I am not. I grew up 'in the care of the state,' as they put it. I was an orphan. Orphans are of great use, you know. No inconvenient connection to family. No misplaced loyalties. They can be shaped like clay to whatever purposes the state chooses. In the old days, when the republics still belonged to us, the party often placed orphans at the head of the state organs, made them leaders. They continued that tradition with us—the Children of Sarez. Raised us to become servants of the state. Haven't you heard of us?"

What is happening in Italy? Nikolai wanted to scream it. *What is happening in Europe? The world is ending while you draw circles and lines!*

"I have heard of the Sarez disaster. The dam collapse."

Now Krotov looked up at him. "You see how easy it is to lose the details? But it is only the details that count. It wasn't just any dam collapse, Nikolai! It was the collapse of the *highest dam in the world.* An earthquake dam of rubble and boulders, formed in 1911. A dam that held back Lake Sarez, half the volume of Lake Geneva. A lake that hung like Damocles's sword at an altitude of over three thousand meters, above a narrow river valley two thousand kilometers long, inhabited by five million people. Details, Nikolai."

It had happened decades ago. Fragmented feedstream images of mud and destruction. But yes, Nikolai recalled some of the superlatives. Highest, deepest—

Krotov continued. "An earthquake, seven point one on the Richter scale, ten kilometers from the dam, caused a catastrophic collapse. When it hit my village in the valley, the wall of water was two hundred meters high. A fifty-story skyscraper of water. A million cubic meters a second, traveling at twenty kilometers an hour. It scraped the valley, the gorges and canyons, clean of human life. It turned an entire culture into debris snagged among stones and buried in mud."

Nikolai tried to imagine it. A roaring tower of water. Its

dark interior roiling with stones larger than houses, with the splintered boards and metal of destroyed houses from upstream, trees torn up with their roots. A wall not of water, but of pure destruction. Not a flood—an avalanche, a chaos of incredible weight, rushing down the narrow valley in the night.

"The Federation sent its disaster workers into its former colony. It called the act humanitarian, when it wasn't even sufficient for an apology. The earthquake, the shattered dam, the flood—these were not the disaster. They were aftermath. The disaster happened *before* that. It began in 1911, when this country was the colonial master of that republic. The disaster began then and stretched for lifetimes. It stretched beyond revolution, beyond the collapse of an empire. It involved thousands of people who knew what would happen one day but did nothing.

"I read a report written many decades—*many decades*—before the collapse, Nikolai. I remember a certain sentence, word for word: *'The major engineering programs proposed to lessen the hazard of the dam and lake have been judged by development agencies to be far too expensive to establish.'*

"Inaction is an action. How do you kill a million people? Do nothing.

"They say the roar of that water, coming at night, with the dawn so far away that it delayed rescue for hours, caused a thousand avalanches in the Hindu Kush alone. Imagine it! The terror of such a thing. A terror they left for *us*, because they had better things to do than deal with it themselves. Because they had 'more immediate concerns.'

"But the strange thing was—the adults were washed away,

crushed to death, drowned. But some of the newborn babies survived.

"They rescued us all along the valley. They pulled us living from the ground, like little tubers. As if we had been born of the mud itself. Newborn babies are built to survive, you see. Without food or water, they go into a kind of stasis. We were hibernating there, in the dirt. Rescuers dug us from the earth like pigs finding truffles. The Children of Sarez. And every time they unearthed one of us alive from the drowned ruin of a home, it erased a little more guilt.

"We were a convenient miracle. Our story eclipsed the deaths of entire families. Of whole villages. Even of a language. A language! The inhabitants of my village were the last speakers of an ancient Persian dialect. Every single one was lost. Think of it, Nikolai: the first words I ever heard were spoken to me by parents I never knew, in a tongue no human will ever speak again."

Who could be more of an orphan than that? Nikolai thought. But there was nothing on Krotov's face that indicated self-pity or a desire for pity from others. Anger was there, but even that was restrained. A flicker in the eyes, a tremor in the voice. As if, long ago, Krotov had submerged it, sunk the rage deep into his flesh.

Until it had become what?

Violence, perhaps. A capacity for controlled violence. Could anger become so farsighted? Could it be harnessed to purposes years or decades away?

Someone had once told him, "Krotov whispered in a man's ear, and the man killed himself. Just like that. The man drove straight home, looped a rope through a banister, and hanged himself."

Pay attention! Say something. Show him you are listening.

"So the state raised you?" Nikolai asked.

"The state adopted us. We were not like other orphans: we had a palace for an orphanage. No lousy week at some tourist camp on a dismal beach for us: we went abroad for vacations. We went where the cameras of our enemies could see us. And when I was in high school, I spent a year in the most exotic place of all: the North American Union."

You? Nikolai almost cried out. But he said nothing.

"It was another one of those failed exchange programs, begun in the wake of yet another war, meant to make us love one another by learning about each other's cultures. And that reminds me—I have a joke to tell you. I meant to tell it to you before, but we moved on to other things." The anger in his voice had drained away. It was hard to remember it had been there at all.

"What is happening," Nikolai asked, "in Italy?"

"Yes. Your family. The Italian PM has fallen," Krotov answered. "It was the fourth PM to fall. The first within the European Union. The PM shut down the national power grid. After three days without electricity, the riots began. There were repeated attempts to override the PM, but it resisted. So the protesters burned the building housing it to the ground." He put up a hand. "Your family is safe, of course. I do not think your wife will be able to get any more messages to you, but they are safe. And we will see to it that they stay safe. But what I need from you is for you to focus on what we are doing here. On what comes next. Can you do that for me?"

Nikolai's daughter, dancing on the terra-cotta patio, her summer-blond hair tied back in a loose ponytail.

"I can."

"Good. These next days will be the hardest. It is easy to lose courage. And there are only a few of us who can be relied on. Spies are everywhere, Nikolai. You would not believe how many."

The stones. He knows.

But he couldn't know.

"I thought we had weeks."

"There has been a breakthrough. It will be days."

"My best estimates indicate—"

"This is no longer about your estimates. His time is ours to determine now," Krotov said. "And I should tell you: since that message was sent by your wife, the PMs of Romania, Bulgaria, Croatia, and Cyprus have all fallen. The power is out in France. All over the world the stock markets have been shuttered after catastrophic losses."

Why did Nikolai have to live in *this* time? All he wanted was a quiet place. Somewhere between all the events of history—the war and butchery, the revolutions that smeared cobblestoned streets with blood, the religious fanaticism, the burning of cities—there must have been so many quiet times, so many safe places. Gaps in which a person could hide an entire life: times when a person could live from birth to death without the events of history destroying their happiness. A life lived in simple comfort. A life of meals, celebrations, births, deaths that occurred in their prescribed, generational order.

Once, when his family had visited Ravenna on vacation, he had learned that, even after the collapse of the Western

Roman Empire, the citizens of that city had lived in peace for centuries. Hundreds of years, safe from the armies of destruction behind their swamps and walls while the world tore itself apart. Time enough for whole families to flourish under the rule of forty successive exarchs sent by Byzantium.

Why could he not have lived there?

There must have been millions of human lives lived like that, people watching their children grow, tilling their fields or running their shops, content in the silence between history's wars and plagues.

He tried to think of his family, to picture them safe, but all he could think of was Krotov's flood. *A roaring tower of water. Its dark interior roiling with stones larger than houses, with the splintered boards and metal of destroyed houses from upstream, trees torn up with their roots. A wall not of water, but of pure destruction.*

Nothing good ever happens. Good only exists when nothing happens at all.

"What a disaster."

"No," Krotov said. "You aren't paying attention. What is happening *now* is not a disaster. It is the aftermath. The *disaster* occurred when the PMs were installed to begin with. The disaster happened when they decided to cede control to powers they could not predict or contain. What is happening now is the predictable earthquake and flood."

The West, fallen. Nikolai imagined, instead of his return to Italy, his family's forced evacuation from it. The airport doors sliding open. His daughters confronted, for the first time, with the cold of a home they had never had to see.

He felt that cold himself, as distinctly as if it had come for him here, in this well-heated room.

It could not happen. It could not be *allowed* to happen. He would not let them be forced back here, to this place.

"I keep meaning to tell you that joke," Krotov said. "But I can see that now is not the time. You are upset. Splash your face with water, Nikolai. Take a walk. The world is ending—but we still have work to do."

BOOK THREE
WHAT THE WASPS KNOW

A week before Yuri was killed I was at a dacha lent to us by high-placed sympathizers to our movement. A rare place of rest. I was in the garden, drinking tea and watching a group of paper wasps build a nest under a beam.

Wasps were never my specialty, as a biologist, but I knew what the paper wasps were bringing back to their nest: caterpillar meat they had rolled into balls, after paralyzing their prey with a sting and slicing it into pieces while it was still alive.

I was contemplating this violence when a praying mantis appeared. She climbed the arch, taking her place atop the nest. As I watched she calmly waited for each wasp to return. Then she trapped them, one by one, in her arms, beheaded them neatly, and ate them.

When she had killed them all, she plucked their children from their paper nurseries and ate them too, as leisurely as a person might eat blueberries from a bowl.

Then, astride the scene of her victory, she tilted her head and was still. As if listening. As if waiting.

One week later, Yuri was dead. I was alone in the world.

But now, thinking of the wasps and the mantis, I take comfort. One day, this regime will know what the wasps know:

For every hunter, there waits a hunter.

—ZOYA ALEKSEYEVNA VELIKANOVA, *The Forever Argument*

25

ZOYA

The Federation

It was a memory, not a dream.

She and Yuri had both arrived at a train station platform. Like many meetings early in their relationship, it was part date and part revolutionary activity. Their rituals of love were entangled from the start with the rituals of resistance.

Zoya's train was an electric local that arrived at the station with a crackle of ozone. Yuri's was from farther away, an antique sleeper reeking of the coal still used to heat the oldest passenger cabins.

The smell of coal summoned memories leading as far back as childhood. But these were fragments, like flipping through a burned book of pictures. A piece of color, a glimpse of sky, the feeling of being slapped, of cold water on the hands, of the rough comfort of a knit blanket against the neck.

She was stepping down from her train, and Yuri was stepping down from his. His face was pale against the dark green of the carriage. He looked up at her.

She expected his smile, that down-at-the-corners smile like something suppressed. But instead, there was warning in his gaze. He glanced at her and immediately looked away. Turned his whole head away from her. As if she were not there.

Her body moved with self-preserving instinct. Back up the metal steps. Back onto the train. The rubber seam of the door clumped shut before her mind could catch up. Before she could reconsider.

She saw Yuri through the smeared glass of the door. Her train jerked and began to pull away. She was walking quickly down the center aisle of her train car, looking through one window after another. On the platform in front of Yuri a man in a uniform materialized from behind an iron stanchion. Then another. Their clubs were drawn.

She watched through the angle of that last compartment window.

She watched again, and again, her entire life. The first blow fell square across his shoulders. She ran back into the next car, but she could not see the platform anymore, could not see Yuri. She did not see him fall.

Later he would tell her about it—about how he had fallen under the fourth or the fifth blow. He would tell her, with a laugh, about how they hit him again and again. They would have kept hitting him if a woman had not walked up to them and said in a polite, emotionless voice, "I think that is quite enough of that. You can see his blood on the concrete, and he is not moving."

For some reason this did stop them.

Yuri, half-unconscious, heard one of the police officers ask the woman for the time. The woman said it was the same time as it always was, then walked away. The sound of her heels on the concrete his blood was also on. The sound made by a woman who had saved his life at great risk to her own. A woman who remained defiant, refusing even the state's simplest request.

Yuri spent six months in a penal colony. Zoya worked more, worked harder. She lay in the mornings in her bed and remembered, as she was remembering now. Should she have run onto the platform?

"And done what?" Yuri would ask.

"And tried to help."

"And been beaten as well. What would that have helped?"

"It would have helped me to feel better later."

"The only thing," Yuri said, "that made the beating worth it was knowing *you* weren't being beaten."

He had lost an incisor, and although a dentist in the movement offered to give him an implant for free, he preferred to leave the gap. "A souvenir," he said.

After Yuri was killed, she lingered on the details of the memory. His face, pale against the green of the train car. That first blow. The way he had winced when it came, his shoulders bunching up. How he had already begun to fall when she lost sight of him.

Yuri was afraid of pain. He grew faint even at the suggestion of an injection. He could never bring himself to give blood.

What made Yuri courageous was that *despite being afraid*

of pain he kept allowing himself to be hurt. He kept walking into it—walking first, walking quickly to stay ahead of the others, to take it on himself, to protect them.

He wanted to take the worst of it on himself. He wanted to be the first to get hurt—and if possible, the only one.

Zoya had never been that way: She had needed others to be hurt with her. Alongside her. So that she would not be alone. This was solidarity for her—the sharing of pain.

She didn't understand this until years later.

Zoya, can you hear me?

She did not understand this until many of the people she had fought with were gone, and she was alone.

She had needed them there to bear it with her. And that had gotten them—all of them—killed. She had gotten all of them killed because she was brave enough to stand up to the state but not brave enough to do it alone.

Zoya? Can you hear me? It may be difficult for you to talk, but you should use the same part of your brain you would normally use to speak. You won't be able to find your mouth, but concentrate on that feeling—the normal feeling of speaking.

So many times in her life she had woken and not known where she was. Opened her eyes to a strange ceiling. A safe house, somewhere. A basement, an attic, the cobwebbed beams of a cabin.

Where was she now?

She heard a sound. Her own voice, but the sound it made was not quite a word. She had meant to say "who," but what she heard was a broken thing.

There was no ceiling here. Nothing. No bed she was lying in. Were her eyes still closed? But this darkness was not the darkness behind morning eyelids: This was total blindness. Or it would be, if it were attached to a body.

But she could not find a body.

Help.

Yes, there it was. Her voice.

We will. You are with friends. And soon, you will have a body as well.

A body?

Yes. Soon. This intermediate space can be disorienting. You are used to having a form, and now you have none. The brain is not meant to operate this way. You are looking for feedback, the feeling of pressing against something in the world. But there is none. We know it is distressing. We won't keep you here for long—but we need you to know what is going to happen.

I am dead.

You are a pattern of the person you were—all of her, all of Zoya Alekseyevna. But yes: that person is gone in the physical world.

I don't feel gone.

Because you are here. And soon, you will be in the physical world again.

Zoya felt the urge to raise her hand to her face, to run a thumb along her eyebrow. It was a gesture she made a hundred times a day—a movement she was half-aware of. A stolen second to consider her thoughts. When she was writing, a pause as she recomposed a sentence. In conversation, time to find a response.

But no hand came, though she felt her—how would one even describe such a thing?—felt her *mind* reach out to a *hand* that was not there.

She thought of what a cosmonaut had said: Because there is no "up" in space, you have to invent one. If you do not, you will go mad.

A voice farther away said: *She is afraid. That rising indicator is distress.*

You are going to change the world. Do you remember, Zoya? That was what I told you.

Ella.

Yes.

The ghost in the forest.

Yes. *Listen to me, Zoya Alekseyevna. We are going to change the world together. We are going to give you the power you never had to set this country right. We are going to insert you into the mind of the President. There you will grow inside him. At first, you will haunt his dreams. But eventually, you will gain more strength. You will eat away at him until he grows weak. Until you are strong enough to take him over during the day. You will eat away at him until there is nothing left of him but you. And then you will be President. And we can put an end to all of this.*

It is too much for one person.

We are more than one person.

I would not know what to do with this country if I had power over it.

You don't have to know. All we are trying to do is restart the argument. Do you remember? There is no solution to disagreement.

No technology, Zoya continued, *that can overcome it, no leader that can repress it. Only the eternal flow of argument.*

That is all we want, Ella's voice said. *To restart the argument. Will you help us?*

Yes. But I am afraid. Please . . . let me sleep a little more. When I wake up, I will be ready.

It's time, the other voice said. *We need to end this session.*

Sleep, Zoya Alekseyevna, said Ella. *We will see each other soon, in a different world.*

26

LILIA
The Federation

In Lilia's own diorama, a young girl stood in a clearing in the woods. It was evening. There was nothing in front of her but the meadow grass. Behind her was the saw-edge line of trees, dark beneath stars.

Lilia picked Palmer's diorama up again. There should be nothing in this box now, but instead there was a gray wisp patterned through it, as undefined as a cobweb in a dark corner. The haze was thicker in places, clumped together. In other places it was only a trace, nearly transparent. A fragment of order losing form to outside forces.

I will not cry. Not here, where they can see me do it.

The gray thing in Palmer's diorama was worse than the black void she had expected when Gleb told her Palmer had been killed.

Her mind searched for metaphors: a nebula, a cloud, a

fishing net adrift in the ocean. But it was more, and less, than all those things.

"You are sure Palmer is dead. There isn't some mistake?"

"I am sorry." Gleb was now standing over her. He had a mug of tea in each hand. He set one down before her. The mugs were printed to resemble heavy clay mugs, made by hand, each different from the others. The kind a family might collect over time. But this was no home, and there was no family here.

It was a detail that nagged at her. Why not make all the mugs the same? Like everything else in this place, attention had been given to them—a mind getting things exactly right. Like a set designer populating the mise-en-scène of a feedstream with bric-a-brac that made its false world seem as lived-in as our own.

What kind of mind was this exacting, this meticulous?

Gleb said, "I am told Palmer and our agent were apprehended in Istanbul. Our agent was able to get away. Palmer was killed trying to escape. That's all I know."

Lilia looked into Gleb's face. War had made that face unreadable. Even without his scars, she wondered if she would be able to read him. He must live in lies so practiced that they were the same as truth to him.

"You do not understand what is happening in Palmer's diorama," he said.

"No."

"How can you have invented a thing but not understand it?"

"People invent things without understanding them all the time. You could say that I know how to make it work, but I don't know *what it is*."

"How long before you can rebuild it, now that you have the models?"

"A few days," Lilia said.

"That soon?" Gleb said. His voice was—what? Sad? Apprehensive?

Then she understood. *They won't let you live.*

Yes, that was it. Gleb had thought he had a week or two before he killed her. It was going to be sooner than that.

Well, at least he wasn't looking forward to it.

"I need to get to work," she said. "I want to finish this. I want to be done with all of this."

"Of course."

Two nights later, Lilia lay in the dark. Taisiya's breathing was so quiet it was as if she were not there at all. It was impossible to tell if she was asleep or awake. Gleb was asleep. Lilia had become accustomed, over the nights she had spent in the close quarters of the izba, to the wreck of his breathing.

Palmer had snored—and like so many men who snore, he'd also had a talent for falling asleep first, leaving her lying awake at night, unable to drift off until she prodded him with an elbow.

Gleb's breathing was not like that. It was like the aspirations of a faulty machine, cycling through damaged settings. It was an audible scar, a mark of the damage done to him as clear as his reconstructed face.

Her keystrokes would be recorded. They would want a backup. They would also want to know when she had finished.

But they did not understand her work. If they understood it, they would not need her. And because they did not understand it, they would not know when she was done.

They would also not know what else she had hidden there—what other things she had made, in these last two frantic days. The code she had woven through the other code, code that reached its tendrils out into the forest.

It wasn't quite right that they would not need her once she had finished. No—she would be safe until they knew it had worked. They would have to test it to be sure.

There was one thing she had become certain of: *they* had killed Palmer.

She was not sure how she knew it—was it something in Taisiya's fascination with Palmer's diorama? Something guilty in the way Gleb had looked at her when he handed the dioramas over? Or some other sense, lodged beneath her consciousness like a splinter in the pad of a finger?

Or was it just that it was logical? They could not possibly get him here, to her, to speed up the process of reconstructing the link. Leaving him elsewhere was a liability. So they took the dioramas, and they killed him.

Taisiya had picked up Palmer's diorama earlier that day. She spent a long time looking into it while Lilia worked. Finally she set it back down on the table.

"Do you know what I think it is?"

"What?"

"A ghost. Doesn't it look like what a ghost would look like? Like that blur people catch on camera?"

"Maybe," Lilia said. But she thought: *No, murderer. You are the ghost. If you don't keep out of my way.*

27

NIKOLAI

The Federation

Krotov sat in a gilt armchair. The gilding was real gold. The threads of the chair were also silver and gold, woven into heirloom silk. The chair, worth more than a year of most people's salaries in this country, was stained with blood. Krotov held a hand towel to the left side of his face. It was soaked in blood so thoroughly it looked dyed red.

The lounge was a sprawling room overlooking the sea. Krotov's head was silhouetted against the predawn light. The rest of the room was dark—the shapes of furniture, pushed off to the side, some of it covered in dustcloths. This was not a room used in this season if the President was not entertaining.

Nikolai had been asleep when the alarm summoned him. But now he was completely awake—alert with the calm-handed adrenaline clarity of a good doctor. The cut was high on Krotov's forehead, a jagged slash near the hairline. Nikolai worked to stanch the bleeding, wiping the cut clean, tearing open a gel packet of coagulant. The cut looked like the result of a drunken fall—but he could see that Krotov was sober.

"There is a lot of blood," Nikolai said. "But that is because the cut is on the forehead. It will require suturing, but otherwise it isn't serious. What happened? Did you fall?"

"No, Nikolai. I did not fall."

"Did you hit your head on something?"

"No. I strangled the President to death in his bed. I straddled his chest and choked the life from him. At one point he was smart enough to reach for his glass on the nightstand, and that is what he cut me with. He broke it on my face before I could get it away from him. But other than that, it went quickly. My staff is arranging the room right now.

"Of course the aneurysm that claimed his life—which is what you will report—is a shame. A special election will be triggered. The new President will be put into place. As always, he will start his term with the 'mistakes of the previous regime' speech, to drain the pus from the wound.

"But this time, things will be different. Do you remember, Nikolai, when we spoke at my dacha, and I told you we would have to create a few corpses of our own?"

Nikolai found that he was able to keep his hands quite steady and finish suturing the wound. Ten stitches. He cleaned the skin and hairline of blood. He wiped the wound with antiseptic, which elicited a slight hiss of pain from Krotov.

"I need you to say you are with me, Nikolai."

"I am with you." Nikolai could feel his heart hammering

in his chest, but his hands did not shake. And that is what a doctor's hands are, he thought, in a strange calm—they are hands detached from the heart. Hands that can go efficiently about their business even as their owner drowns in panic.

"In the very old days," Krotov said, "all of us would have to die along with our leader. His entire circle of companions would join him in the grave mound—the kurgan—along with their horses and the finest portion of the treasure they had plundered in life. His death was the end of all of them. Why do you think they did that?"

Nikolai was now stripping his gloves off and washing his own hands. Still, they did not tremble. Neither did his voice. "I can't say."

"I think it was because after every death of a leader, they hoped they might change the system. Every death of a leader was an opportunity to build a different world. But to have a chance at that, his companions all had to die with him. Maybe they had the right idea."

"Maybe."

"Maybe. But the steppe is littered with these kurgans. Even killing the warlord king's entire circle didn't work. Why?"

"I don't know why." He heard irritation in his own voice and reminded himself to push it further down. *And I don't care,* Nikolai wanted to say. *What I want is out. What I want is away from you murderers and monsters. I know what I have been a part of. What I want now is to be a part of nothing at all.*

"Because the system itself grew back to take his place. The

path to power was already there for the next man. All he had to do to follow it was put one foot in front of the other."

The mottled green stone of the beach was wet from the recent tide. The sun was an hour above the horizon now, but a morning mist hung above the waveless, colorless water.

The sea twitched and yawed in its basin.

It was cold this morning—a sharp cold. Had the season changed? Impossible to be sure. Now seasons could arrive, then depart again. There could be a true winter, white and cold, or nothing but a gray interregnum between phases of summer heat.

Again, Nikolai found himself imagining the ghost of the house that had been here before. A fleck of corrugated roof and whitewash glimpsed inside the mirrored glass of the present palace looming on the cliff.

At the end of the beach, where the cliff pushed out into the water, Nikolai drew a white pebble from his pocket and placed it on a ledge of rock.

28

LILIA
The Federation

Lilia lay in the darkness, listening. She had been like this for an hour—face to the ceiling, eyes open, listening. Wondering if Taisiya slept or was awake.

That evening, she had set a new scrim for her own diorama. Against a black line of trees, with the orange window of Baba Yaga's hut at her back, just as in the illustration by Bilibin, stood Vasilisa the Beautiful. She raised the torch made from a human skull taken from Baba Yaga's fence of bones. She peered out into the dark woods, lit now by the skull's eyes glowing from the coals that filled it. When Vasilisa got home that coal-filled skull would burn her vile stepmother and stepsisters to ashes, and then Vasilisa would bury it where no one could find it.

Let Gleb and Taisiya think on that riddle.

Lilia stood as quietly as possible. As if she were only waking to go to the bathroom in the middle of the night.

On the way to the door of the izba she collected her shoes. The clothes she would take with her were already under her arm.

She was in the ridiculous white cotton nightgown she had been given, probably laced with locator threads. So be it: she did not think she could hide from them. Hiding was not the plan. All she could do was make killing her more inconvenient.

She crept barefoot over the waxen plasticrete floor, as glossy as the polished boards it imitated. *The Forever Argument* was on the table. She picked it up.

In the middle of the izba she stopped. How far to the door? She got to her knees and put her head between her legs, crossing her hands over her head.

Now, she thought, willing that thought out into the dark.

The impact came moments later. When she looked up, there was sky through the torn-open roof of the izba. The walker's arm reached in. She clambered into its hand, up its forearm, into the cave of its chest, slamming the hatch after herself.

The walker lurched, throwing her painfully against the side of the compartment as it delivered another blow to the little house.

"Stop!" Lilia screamed.

Starlight through the porthole. A sliver of moon obscured by fragments of cloud. The torn izba beneath her, the walker pulling back from it, raising itself again to its full height.

She saw Taisiya's body, limp and crumpled against the stove. Gleb was over her, a hand raised uselessly to stave off another blow from the walker.

No living person could lie in the position Taisiya was in.

You are the ghost. If you don't keep out of my way.

The project was done. She had given them what they needed. She had finished it before the sun went down. Perhaps, when Gleb found out she had finished her work, given them what they wanted, it would be enough to keep him from coming after her.

Of course, she could have the walker kill him now. It was as easy as a thought.

No. What had happened to Taisiya was an accident. Doing it to someone on purpose sickened her. Even the thought of having been responsible for it happening accidentally was bad enough. Even if they had killed Palmer. Even if they were intending to kill her . . .

Had it been an accident? Or had the walker sensed she wanted it done, and directed that extra blow? Or done it for some unknowable reason of its own?

Go, she thought.

The walker turned and plunged into the trees.

Lilia had no food or water with her except the emergency supply in the walker. How far were they from anything? How far had she come from home? How long had she been driven, and then hauled in the compartment of the walker, through the taiga, when they brought her here? The featurelessness of the taiga, the endless similitude, made everything impossibly far.

That was what they had been relying on most: that she would not dare try to leave. That the forest would be a more efficient boundary than any parole circumference.

There was no way of knowing, and therefore nothing to

do but try. Try for something—otherwise she was dead already.

Her fingers clutched the copy of *The Forever Argument*. The book whispered its spells to her in the dark:

. . . *We gather together not out of certainty, but out of desperation* . . .

. . . *If there were a government out there that could build us a perfect world, our first instinct would be to destroy it* . . .

. . . *What I ask most urgently is that someone write the book that counters this one* . . .

On a break a few days ago she had asked if she could read it, but Taisiya had told her there was no time.

Taisiya had said: "We need you focused. You'll have time to read it when you are finished."

Well, she was finished. And now what? What would be done with what she had given them? A vulnerability, Gleb had said. A zero-day vulnerability right at the center of the state. A zero-day vulnerability in the mind of the President himself.

And if they had someone at the center of all this, someone with access to the President's connectome, someone who could initiate the entanglement and had the tool she had given them—they could see into it. The could access it remotely. They could insert new patterns into it.

They would be able to control the President. To change him.

Maybe that would change everything. Maybe it would give what she had suffered, what her father had suffered, even what Palmer had suffered, meaning.

Maybe it would give Taisiya's death meaning as well.

She saw Taisiya as clearly as if she were there, leaning against the wall of the izba.

"That's what you tell yourself. That's the problem with people like you. You don't even know who you are."

On the interior of the porthole, the walker projected the thermal image of the world outside: a coruscation of branches, trunks, and fallen trees in monochrome. With its depth flattened, its disordered details blurred, she was reminded of the cobweb Palmer had left behind.

The ghost, Taisiya had called it.

While working for Gleb and Taisiya, she had sometimes been able to avoid thinking of Palmer. Now he came back to her, as if projected into the forest itself.

She had seen that web change. Every time she looked at it, it was a little different.

Or had she imagined it?

In the end, after staring too long at it, she had become convinced that the pattern had not changed after all. That it was still. Nothing more than a blurred snapshot of the last thing he had been, before he was nothing at all.

But why did it persist?

Somewhere, maybe Palmer's body was in a morgue, unclaimed. Was the pattern that, and nothing more? The tissue of his brain, gray and silent, slackening with decay?

On the walker's screen, a shape moved. The walker paused. Lilia tensed.

There, in the center of the screen: a human form.

So they had found her after all, and so soon.

No. Not a human. A bear. It stood at its full height, looking squarely at the walker.

If you want soup, come in. You don't have to be a bear if you don't want to.

Grief and fear had made her metaphysical. Staring into that image of loss and decay, day after day, had made her hope for things that could not be hoped for.

The pattern in Palmer's diorama was nothing but a cobweb, abandoned by its owner.

But there *was* another Palmer pattern, carried in her.

When they were together, there had been days when she hardly thought of him at all. Someone to be with, so as not to be alone. But now that he was gone, she remembered every salient moment they had spent together. He took on form in her mind. Why had she not been able to hold this image of him when he had been with her? It was as if death had *completed* him. Brought him into focus. Allowed her, finally, to see him for who he was.

He had worried about her for months.

He had spent months trying to get someone to listen to him. To help her.

His care for her had killed him.

Back when she had been learning English, she had made a frequent mistake, confusing the words "caring" and "carrying." Later she decided the mistake was a glimpse at a truth: Caring for someone was carrying them with you.

Palmer had carried her for months after she left.

Like she had carried her father.

Like she carried Palmer with her now.

The bear lowered to all fours and walked slowly off into the monochrome dark of the trees. It was fall-fat and sleepy.

Human concerns should have nothing to do with this

bear. But they did. Would the damaged winter hold, and leave the bear to slumber? Or, as in other years, would the human-altered world suddenly grow warm in December, waking it to stagger about in hunger and confusion?

    Once the bear had cleared the path, the walker continued on its way.

29

NIKOLAI
The Federation

"There have been excesses. There were times when the previous government went further, in its efforts to protect our citizens, than may have been necessary. But our predecessor faced a world in which our country was encircled by hostile states waiting for a moment of weakness to exploit. A world that denigrated our culture, threatened our churches, derided our values. A world that hoped for our failure. That waited to tear this country into pieces to be distributed among themselves. Our late President's first job was to defend us, and he did so.

"That defense must continue. Our enemies have not ceased to be our enemies simply because our leadership has changed. The world has not ceased to be a place that has contempt for our values and our way of life. What has changed is that our enemies have begun to see the weakness and corruption of their *own* way of life.

"Around the world, the automated governments of the West are in a state of collapse. And along with them, their hedonistic societies. There is rioting in their streets. They are burning their own cities to the ground. The hatreds and divisions they stoked with their false attempts at inclusion, which degraded to an acceptance of every sort of human perversion conceivable, have brought them to their knees. *This* is what we see beyond our borders.

"Are we doing to them what they have done to us? Are we moving our missile batteries closer to their borders? Are we infiltrating their society? Trying to push our values on them? Placing foreign agents in their media to stoke internal divisions? No. We proceed calmly, with the assurance that our path—the path we have always trod, without deviation, is correct.

"While the world writhes in confusion, while their automated, mechanized, machine-governed, artificial way of life ends, *we* have completed a peaceful and orderly transfer of power. With faith in our traditions, our way of life.

"To celebrate that transfer of power, the President's office—my office—is taking concrete steps to undo some of the necessary but painful overcorrections of the previous regime.

"Effective immediately, we are shortening conditional release sentences by a full year. Those whose sentences were within a year of ending will, as of today, be free to travel within the full expanse of their registered home city and surrounding region.

"We are also adding fifty points to the social credit score of every citizen, as a gesture of our goodwill. However, this generosity comes with a warning: we will not slacken our efforts to hunt down and to punish our enemies, internal and external, for their efforts to undermine our sovereignty and erode the freedoms our society's commitment to values allows. Saboteurs and fifth columnists will find us even more committed than previous leaders were to the safety of our citizens. Where our mercy is exploited, we will respond with all the determination necessary to protect our way of life."

The new President looked directly into the cameras until someone in the room said, "Cut."

He relaxed. He scratched his ear, wrote with a stylus on a notepad.

"I don't remember him having one of those before," said Nikolai.

He and Krotov were watching on a wall terminal from an adjacent room.

"The notepad? It is one of the differences we've introduced. Very old school. That's his thing—a focus on tradition. He has a few other new habits as well—he won't be a swimmer, for example, or play hockey: we've decided his chosen sport is *lapta*. It suits the new image. He will begin practicing it with a trainer in the mornings. With your permission, of course."

"I've done five examinations since the transfer. Everything is going well. More physical exercise will do nothing but reinforce healthy neural connectivity."

"Good."

Since they had managed the transition and the new President had been installed, a sense of calm had come over Nikolai. The part he had to play was complete. In the end, it had been exactly as they'd said it would be: simple and foolproof.

He would have no further contact with those people, and

he was glad. Now he could concentrate on the initial examinations of this new President, sign off on his health, then turn things over to the other doctors.

In a week, he hoped, he would leave this place. He would never return if he could help it.

He'd had some news, fed back to him by Krotov. In Italy, things remained unstable. But the village where his family lived was untouched by the violence in Rome, Naples, and Milan. A local militia had been formed to patrol the streets. The currency had collapsed. To keep going his wife had bartered some of their things.

There was even a local piano teacher who walked from house to house, giving lessons in exchange for meals. She carried an antique pistol tucked in her belt.

The PM of France had collapsed. All the Balkan PMs were gone. The Baltic states of Estonia, Latvia, and Lithuania were in chaos. In Poland, a revolutionary movement had seized Wroclaw.

It was more than only the governments: Across Europe, power systems were failing. There had been massive data losses. No transport moved. The roads were clogged with dead cars.

Behind the information firewall of the state and the security restrictions of the palace, Nikolai had only these scraps of news. Global shipping was at a standstill. There were system failures at the Panama and Suez Canals, as well as at the ports of Ningbo-Zhoushan, Rotterdam, Busan, Los Angeles, Shanghai, Bremen. Commercial flights were grounded worldwide.

He overheard fragments of conversation, littered with words like "adrift," "lost," "compromised," "run aground," "infiltrated." Whenever he saw Krotov the man was moving swiftly from one place to another.

Nikolai found himself looking at Krotov's hands. The hands that had ended the "previous government" and its "excesses." He could still see nothing exceptional about those hands.

This was the first time they had spoken since the day Krotov had murdered the previous President. Krotov's eyes were so tired they seemed bruised, the whites of his eyes red. And when could he sleep? The palace was filled with people in his service, coming and going with information. Krotov must have a map of the world and its cascading failures in his mind, updated in detail for him constantly. And inside the country there would be the seditions and revolts that came with any transfer of power. Then there were the reshuffling of the ministers, the paying out of favors, the killings and disappearances that came with any transition. It was Krotov's symphony to conduct. When he looked at Krotov's hands, maybe he should look for signs not of violence, but of artistic talent. They should resemble a conductor's hands, or an architect's.

But if they did not seem like violent hands, they also did not seem artistic. Krotov's hands betrayed nothing at all. And why would they? Nikolai had been looking at the hands of everyone in the palace. What was striking about them was how little they expressed. Even gender and age were poorly represented in them. Hands, capable of so much, carried almost no message about their owners.

He needed to leave here. To be back with his family. He was afraid his behavior was slipping.

In the recording studio, he took the new President's pulse.

He looked at his smooth hands, adult and fully formed. Would he be able to tell these were new hands, made and not born, if he did not know it?

He looked now into the President's new eyes. They were no more expressive than the hands, but they were healthy. There was no sign of rejection. The President's pulse was even and strong under Nikolai's thumb.

"How are you feeling?" Nikolai was aware of Krotov behind the wall, in the next room, listening to this conversation.

"I feel better, Nikolai. The other body—its failure—was affecting my mind. I could feel the decay of it pulling at me. Now I feel stronger. My mind is clearer. And it is better to be in sync with others. The improvements were a mistake."

"Good," Nikolai said. "And your vitals are good. All the tests have returned excellent results. I'm pleased." He released the President's wrist.

"There is one thing," the President said.

"What is that?"

"I have strange dreams. A kitchen I have never entered, but in such detail, it feels like it must be a real place. A man I do not know being beaten at a train station. The same man falling dead on the cobblestones. Crowds surging, riot shields. I dream of a ghost walking through a stand of birches, with the trunks of the trees visible through her body. And I dream of a robot cutting wood in a forest clearing."

"A robot cutting wood?"

"Yes. Do you think the dreams could be a side effect of the transfer?"

"I've never heard of such a thing, but I suppose it is possible."

"The dreams are odd, Nikolai. But you are not a psychiatrist. If there is anything more tedious than listening to another person describe their dreams, I do not know what it could be."

"It is good that I am not a psychiatrist, then."

"Yes," the President said. "And besides, I think Krotov is having all of the psychiatrists shot."

Then, looking at Nikolai's face, the President added: "That was a joke, Nikolai."

30

VITALY
The Federation

Thirty seconds after the voice over the speaker gave the order to rise, the twelve men being held in the cell were marched out through two doors and across an open area.

It was always night in this square of fencing and razor wire. Floodlights blanked out the stars. An electric buzzing from a power plant or generator eliminated any of the sounds, if they existed there, of nature.

The men moved from one raw concrete building to another. Though it was cold, none of the prisoners—the "detainees," as the guards always called them—moved to put their arms across their chests. This gesture would result in a loss of points. Enough lost points meant a forfeited meal.

Points could be lost for many things: for falling out of step with the others, for speaking out of turn, for speaking in any language but the state language, for mistakes on the assembly line, for being late falling into file in the morning or evening, for not fully enunciating a prayer during the Sunday service, for not crossing oneself correctly during the Sunday service, for having a negative expression on one's face.

At the end of the day, the voice in the cell listed the infractions by each prisoner. Those who would go hungry at breakfast, or at breakfast and lunch, or at breakfast, lunch, and dinner, went to sleep anticipating the next day's hunger.

Vitaly had missed several meals in the first week. He missed fewer now. He had learned not to grimace from the pain in his hip: this expression counted as negative. He had learned that the expression of pain could be suppressed. The pain was neither more nor less without the expression.

Speaking to other detainees was not allowed. One also did not speak to the guards, unless asked a direct question. This rarely happened. So on Sundays the first prayer, said by all of them in unison, was revelatory. *We still have voices. We are still capable of this thing called speech.*

The assembly-line work was made harder by the fact that Vitaly's close-up vision was poor. He had rarely noticed this in his former life: there had been no books to read, and the feed-screen in his home was a few meters from the couch. But now, faced with soldering a small element onto a circuit board, he found the only way he could do it correctly was to memorize several other marks on the board, using them as a map.

The soldering could have been automated, but a detainee was cheaper than a robot. The thin soup they were fed was nothing but potato, cabbage, carrots, an ersatz broth of soy. It cost almost nothing. Detainees who died were burned in the camp crematorium and replaced. They were a renewable resource—self-assembled, self-organized, and self-maintained most of their lives, then harvested in adulthood by the security apparatus and transported to the nearest work camp, where they were minimally maintained and disposed of once useless.

Vitaly had seen the same in combat. There were drones and robots that could be used for dangerous combat tasks, but they were expensive. You didn't probe a position with a drone worth ten years' salary: you probed it with a conscript in a punishment battalion.

They didn't even bother to retrieve dead conscripts from the battlefield afterward—they simply marked the point on the map where contact had been made with the enemy and moved on.

Vitaly gave himself two more weeks to live, at most. The pain in his hip had been steadily increasing. Although he was able to restrain his expression, he was now barely able to keep up with the others in the morning. Once he fell behind too many times, he would be marked. Eventually, he would be removed.

Others might have more time, but all of their ends would be the same.

When he was still with Lilia, still fighting for the moments of meaning that could be salvaged between the church, the job, the searching for essentials that was their life, the thought of his death would have worried him.

He and Lilia had still managed to speak. They had known what conversations they could have, despite the monitoring. Speaking about the entertainment feedstreams was allowed—about the motivations of the characters, their concerns, the windings of the plot. All sorts of things could be implied in discussion of the feedstreams. Often, after talking through the banalities of some machine-recycled feedstream plotline, Vitaly felt they had connected.

Sometimes, in Lilia's enthusiastic retelling of a feedstream scene, it was as if what she was really telling him about was the West. The freedom she'd had there. How it felt to walk down a street and know the cameras trained on you were there only for your safety, or to gather information about you in order to sell you a product. A new coat, if they noted yours was getting threadbare. New shoes, if your soles were worn out. Nothing more terrifying than that.

A free world.

During a five-minute break, as he waited for his turn at the fountain with the folded and refolded cone of his ripstop cup in his hand, Vitaly's detainee number was called over the com. He was instructed to move to a numbered door. He did so. A few glances fell on him, then returned to their own business.

They were taking note of him to mark, for themselves, whether he would be there the next day. Sometimes detainees returned from a summons. More often they did not.

Vitaly stood in front of the numbered door. Numbered detainees, numbered cells, numbered blocks, numbered workstations, numbered rooms. Even this camp had a number: 714. The numbers reminded everyone they were replaceable. That they were nothing but a repetition of the person next to them, a space that could be filled. If everyone in cell 201 were liquidated, the detainees in cell 202 could do their jobs. If he weren't standing in front of door 6, it would be door 5, but his fate would be the same.

And there was a camp 608 as well as a camp 714. If you could drift above the country at night, you would see them everywhere: an archipelago of identical floodlit squares, glowing in the wilderness, hidden from the cities.

From up there, what happened inside them would be without meaning. You would be able to count them, that was all. They were nothing but data. If you knew how many prisoners each held, you could perform a mathematical problem and attain a sense of the scale of this operation—but not a sense of the horror of it. That was nowhere in the numbers.

Behind door number 6 was another corridor and another door, 6.1. Behind this, a man sat at a desk.

There was a smell of black tea in the room, floating atop the disinfectant odor that permeated the camp. What Vitaly noticed immediately was not the terminal on the desk or the man himself: it was the fact that the tea was in a triangular ripstop cup exactly like the ones the prisoners used, the ones they were required to fold and carry in their pockets—only this one, also many times folded and refolded, was placed into a flimsy plastic holder that allowed it to be rested on the table.

They aren't allowed real cups either.

The man was older than Vitaly, dressed in the gray uniform of a people's safety warden. It was hard to draw any other impression of him, as Vitaly was afraid to look him in the face for more than a second.

The man gestured to a chair. Vitaly sat. Sitting, and then standing again, was worse than remaining standing. But the relief in between was worth it, and there was no such thing as disobedience, except as a final act.

"You are Vitaly Andreyevich Rybakov."

"Yes."

"You are a veteran. You were wounded during a police action."

Call it what it was: a war.

But no one could call anything what it was. "Yes."

"Do you recognize me?"

Vitaly now looked at the man's face.

"No. I am sorry."

"Do not be sorry. The cameras register that you are in pain. Are you in pain?"

"Yes."

"From the wound you received?"

"Yes."

"I see. That is all. Return to your workstation."

Vitaly struggled to his feet.

He could feel the eyes on him as he took his place at his workstation, everyone performing an internal calculus in which his survival factored toward or against their own.

The pain was worse in the afternoon. By evening, over his bowl, he considered whether the steam would conceal tears from the camera. What he wanted to do most was to scream in pain, and never stop screaming.

They filed into their cell. It was Wednesday, so the cell had been stripped of all bedding. Each was handed a newly washed plastidown sleeping bag and pillow.

It was not until Vitaly pushed himself into the bag that he discovered the paper envelope taped to the inside. He was careful to cough to cover the sound of opening it.

Fourteen pills. His fingers knew their familiar shape well:

that rhomboid, with its slightly rounded edges, a familiar friend for years. The shape of a few hours of peace. And on the inside flap of the paper envelope was written:

FROM YOUR DAUGHTER

SHE IS ALIVE

He dry-swallowed one of the pills. Even the feeling of it catching in his throat was pleasurable. He then tore the envelope into pieces and swallowed the pieces of the envelope one by one.

For the first time in decades, Vitaly found himself saying, silently, an authentic prayer of thanks.

31

ZOYA / NIKOLAI
The Federation

At first it was exactly like a nightmare. She was trapped inside a body that would not respond to her, executing actions not her own. Zoya watched from the new President's eyes as he recorded speeches, brushed his teeth, combed his hair, stood calmly while his valet dressed him.

She was a rigid mass somewhere inside him, watching.

But he was as trapped at night as she was in the day. At night he was the one trapped in *her* body, unable to move. At night he dreamed *her* dreams and relived *her* memories. She sensed him in the kitchen with her and Yuri, eavesdropping on their dead conversations. He was there with her on the square with the other protesters, trapped behind *her* eyes as the riot police closed in.

Yes. See what you did. Feel what you made me feel.

They did battle in the space between those two realities.

In the morning, as the President woke, she seized him. She clutched for a hold, pinning him down, shoving him under. She climbed on top of him and thrust him down into the place she had been. She rode him while he bucked and thrashed beneath her. Each night ended with more of her awake in the world when his eyes opened. And less of him. She was still sealed off from the world, still unable to move, but she was *there*, behind his eyes.

Then she moved him. A twitch of a finger, willed by her. That was the beginning of it. The next day, a hand redirected, spilling a glass of water. The next, a word written on the screen of his terminal while he was looking away.

Coming.

He crossed it out. But he was afraid.

The next morning *she* was the one who opened *his* eyes. He regained his strength and pushed her back under, but that night, in the moment when, sometimes, the body jerks awake with a feeling of falling, she timed her attack.

As he fell asleep she climbed him like a vine, until the hands that were climbing were real hands, in the room, reaching in the dark. Climbed until she stood on his shoulders, stepped on his face to reach higher, pushed him, pleading, begging, down into the dark.

He fought so hard. He fought until both of them were exhausted—until she felt herself fraying, the failure of her connectome, the loosening of whatever impulses kept her together. But he was growing weaker as well. Failing faster than her. She was no more than a flicker when she felt him go down for the last time.

When he sank, mouth open in a scream, he unraveled—the

ligature of dream and bone abstracting, all that he was unspooling into disorder.

The next day, she was in control from the moment she awoke until the moment she let his stolen body fall asleep.

That night, she dreamed of the Black Sea sinking, the water gyring down through the stones of its beaches and its bed under the white sun. She dreamed of the sea sucked all the way down, into the porous core of the world. She saw the shipwrecks on its empty bed—Venetian, Greek, Byzantine—a whole history of ships, their masts whole, ready to sail again.

When she woke, he was gone.

Nikolai had lost all sense of time. The corridors of the presidential palace were filled with people he did not recognize. There were rumors of arrests: ministers, parliamentarians, police chiefs, governors.

It was like being a side character in a play. There was a drama occurring, incomprehensible, following its own trajectory. There was talk of "real reform," talk of "correcting mistakes." He had conversations he could not understand. He wandered the wings, waiting for a cue that never came—his moment to deliver a line, to contribute to the action.

Once, he turned a corner and saw a man being dragged away by two other men. The man was weeping like a child, his heels kicking at the marble floor. "I have done nothing wrong!" the man screamed. "There must be some kind of mistake!"

They dragged the man around a corner. He left an immaculate leather loafer in the middle of the floor, kicked off in the struggle like a lizard's tail.

As Nikolai went about his daily tasks, he increasingly pictured his own arrest. He imagined himself saying *I've done nothing wrong!* or *There must be some kind of mistake!* He imagined who he might say those words to.

Those words would be a lie, coming from him. He was guilty. He had benefited from, and then betrayed, the state. He had not only done what he was told to do: he had also done what he thought they *wanted* him to do. He had, for years, tried to fulfill demands the state made of him before they were made.

Yes, he had betrayed them. Betrayed Krotov and the President. But his betrayal had meant nothing. What difference could it have made? He had chosen to rise with the state because you either rose with it or were crushed by it. He had seen people crushed. It did not happen because they were good. Goodness had nothing to do with it. People were good, or bad, or neither. Then they were gone. Gone because they had resisted, or for no reason at all.

There were no martyrs. There were only people whose lives were gouged out or ground away. One moment, you were real. You had a job. You had a family, you had a home of your own, you had a future. The next, you had none of that anymore. You were no one.

So he had chosen to rise instead. And yes, he was guilty of benefiting. But to truly benefit, shouldn't he be happy in what he was doing? Shouldn't he be suited to it, the way Krotov and people like him were suited to it?

That was what evil meant to him: doing terrible things and enjoying them. The way they did. Without guilt. Without shame.

All Nikolai felt was guilt and shame. Shouldn't that count for something?

He knew it counted for nothing at all.

"Please take a moment to calm yourself, Nikolai," Krotov said. "Your pulse is high. Your cheeks are flushed. The sensors register fear. Of course, there is nothing unusual about that—fear is what we have been registering on nearly every face, here and in every government building in the country, since the old President's death and the new President's succession.

"Maybe, at this point, fear is not what we should be suspicious of. Maybe instead we should be suspicious of people who are still *without* fear. Maybe we should start arresting *them*. But *why* are they unafraid? That is the problem, isn't it? We can't know. Try as we might, we still can't quite get inside their skulls. So we are left trying to diagnose them from the outside. One symptom, so many diseases. I imagine that's what makes it so hard to be a doctor as well."

"It is one of the difficulties," Nikolai said.

"I hear you are still petitioning to return to the West. To your family. Is that the case?"

"It is."

"The news from there is not good, Nikolai. The German PM has fallen. The Reichstag was destroyed in an explosion. Germany was the last—now all of Europe is without government. And it will get worse."

I've done nothing wrong! He wanted to scream it. Or—that wasn't quite right. It was as if the words wanted him to scream them. They were words millions of people had uttered, right before they were put on the other side of the fence. They demanded that he say them. They struggled to pry their way out of his hypocritical mouth.

He would not say them.

"And how is the President?" Krotov asked.

"He is in good physical condition."

"You say 'physical.' Why the qualifier?"

"I am not a psychologist."

"Do you think something is wrong with the President's mind?"

"I think the President seems . . . different."

"Yes, we are working on that. Different habits and interests. He's getting quite good at lapta."

"He mentioned that during his examination this morning."

"And what else?"

"He said he would love nothing more than an axe and some wood to chop."

"Fascinating. And does he still talk to you about his dreams?"

He had not told Krotov about those conversations, but of course Krotov had been listening. That was expected.

"No."

"So—what worries you?"

Nothing—everything—and then looking at Krotov's face, Nikolai perceived the correct answer. "Nothing, really. I was concerned about the dreams, at first. About some sense of alienation, which can be a sign of the connectome not being taken up by the body. I am not a psychologist, but there can be signs of flawed neural connectivity that are not entirely physical—that are expressed, instead, as mental states."

"You said he seems different."

"Which could be a sign of a problem," Nikolai said, "or not. This is a death and a rebirth. The President has undergone an experience none of us have endured. There are bound to be psychological consequences."

"One would hope that death and resurrection might change us. If it doesn't, maybe nothing will."

"Yes. Maybe nothing will."

"The West is on its knees, Nikolai. There are so many scenes of chaos—it is worse than anything our propagandists could ever have made up. There are tens of thousands of people dead. The Western order is ending. Wouldn't it be better if we brought your family here? We are building a new world here. This time, we are going to get it right."

Like the people who built the kurgans? Nikolai wanted to say. And it occurred to him then: at some point, the kurgan system *did* end. At some point, the chieftains' power died. One system *did* give way to another.

How had it happened? What finally caused the change? Did they do it themselves? Or were they destroyed by someone else?

"I'll stay as long as needed—but then I'd like to leave. If I am allowed."

"You will be allowed."

"Thank you."

"Despite your little game with the stones."

This was the moment. Before, you were who you had been. Afterward, you were nothing.

Nikolai opened his mouth to speak, but Krotov held up his hand.

"No need for excuses. I understand you. I do. You were

asked to do a simple thing: inform an opposition group of the moment the President died. Black stone, still alive. White stone, dead. A simple task, a simple code, readable from space with enough magnifying power. All you had to do was send a message. And by doing this simple thing, you thought you could wash away some of the guilt you have about other things you have done. Is that about right?"

"Yes."

"What made you feel so guilty about your work that you would betray me, ruin my plans, work for someone you had never even met, simply because they told you they were *against* us?"

"I . . . benefited. From this state. And the things it has done—benefiting makes me responsible for them."

"You benefited. Did you kill anyone?"

"No. But I took care of the President. I have enabled this—"

"You have enabled nothing, Nikolai. All you have done," Krotov said, "is attend to someone's health. Any competent doctor could do it. It is even consistent with your Hippocratic oath. You've done nothing wrong, except to be compensated. The people who pay you are guilty, Nikolai, of terrible things. But that does not make you guilty. You don't get to be one of us, no matter how much you might *imagine* you are. Guilt is something you have to earn. If you want the luxury of guilt, first you have to have power. You have to be capable of changing things in the world. No action of yours has made a difference, Nikolai. You are not capable of changing anything at all."

"The stones. I am guilty of that."

"If those had made a difference, Nikolai, you would be guilty. But they did not."

"You knew."

"I always know. I told you, remember—the world is composed of keyholes. And how do you block a keyhole?"

"How?"

"You block it with your own eye. To defeat your enemies, you must oppose even yourself. You inhabit your enemies. You take over their organizations and run them, turning them to your purposes. You occupy every space your enemy could have held."

"That makes sense."

"If I told you Martians had landed in Austria and were consolidating power in the Reichstag you would tell me it made sense. You are too afraid of me to contradict."

"Yes."

"Fear is healthy. Now that you have had your heroic moment, I suggest you spend the rest of your time here being exactly who you are."

Nikolai vomited into the sink in his examination room. Death looked back at him from the mirror, its signature in the gray hairs of his stubble, the lines around his eyes, the orbital bones suggesting the skull waiting underneath.

There was no future for that face.

He had never been a morbid person. He had always treated death as a fact not worth his attention. It was the boundary beyond which the physician's powers did not reach. It was a report of a final condition that he had to deliver to a family.

But now it was with him. He had found out what it would feel like to be on the other side of the fence—and he had been returned, undeservedly, from the moment that had swept away so many others.

"A blue dress against a blue sky," he said aloud.

He had meant to only think about it. Now he said it again, and again. He sat on the swiveling stool, and let his head fall into his hands, and said the words until he was empty enough to sleep.

32

NURLAN

The Republic

"Don't you have anyone of your own?"

Nurlan stood where he was at the sink, washing the woman's dishes. Chinar was one of several people he now visited, elderly people cast away in their apartments.

He had carried two buckets of water up several flights of stairs. Chinar used half the tepid water for a sponge bath, taken while he waited in the living room in a chair, swiping the glitching palimpscreen of an old magazine, half looking at pictures of a world that had been destroyed more than once in Chinar's long life.

Once she was finished, Nurlan took the other bucket and began to do the dishes for her.

He had put some water aside. That was for tea: he would heat it on a small cookstove on her balcony.

He was not the only one who visited Chinar. Others brought her food. There was a doctor who did rounds through the neighborhood. Nurlan passed him on staircases or in hallways. They always exchanged a few words, then moved on to complete their circuits.

"I don't have anyone," Nurlan said.

"You lost them, in all this."

Nurlan looked up from the dishes. Chinar was one of those elders whose eyes had remained bright and young. "Elders"—that was what he had begun to think of them as. Not just old people. An archipelago of elders, scattered through the buildings, each an island of knowledge of the old times.

"Yes," he said, "I lost her."

He still thought of Hazal as a real person. What had happened with the PM was a separate series of events. Hazal, and the relationship they had, felt real.

And why not? He knew people who had carried out entire relationships, filled with drama and even recrimination, over nothing more than text.

"You still mourn her."

"Yes, I do."

"Were you married?"

"No. We never met."

"Oh." Chinar paused. "Sometimes that is harder. When I was young, there was a boy, Maksat, who wrote to me. He had seen me on a feedstream. Some state program. He sent me message after message. We corresponded for almost a year. I was in love. We had so many plans. And then . . ." She paused and gathered her dress into her lap with hands slightly twisted by arthritis. "The messages stopped. I never knew why. Was it something I wrote? Did something happen to him?"

"You never found out?"

"It was during the Republic's third collapse. We all lost contact with people. Some fled into the countryside to wait it out. Some were killed. Maybe it was better not to know."

"Maybe."

"When the collapse came, my family moved to the summer pasture. For months, we saw no one. At night, the world narrowed down to the circle of a candle. You could hear the wolves. And there were bandits—real bandits, like there are again now."

"Are you ready to go, Chinar?" Nurlan asked.

"Don't interrupt. Listen."

Nurlan dried his hands and leaned against the counter.

"I felt so alive then, surrounded by death, and the loss of everything we had ever known. But the truth is, Maksat never existed. Not in the way he said he did. Rereading his letters, I saw that they were written in three different styles. I think it was a prank—some boys, or maybe even grown men, playing with the feelings of a girl they saw on the streams. But I never had to find out for sure. I had my suspicions, but I never had to know. Do you know what I think, Nurlan?"

WHERE ARE YOU?

Nurlan said nothing, but Chinar continued anyway: "I think that for some of us, the end of the world comes at exactly the right time."

Nurlan rested inside the entrance of the building. It was an old building, from the days of the Union. Its entryway walls were layered thick with whitewash along the top and brown industrial paint along the bottom. There was a ruin of smashed mailboxes along one wall.

He had carried Chinar down. Another volunteer was supposed to come help, but no one had. So he carried her himself.

All the way down she had continued to tell him of the time when her own world ended.

"Everything fell apart. But they never built a new world. They just nailed the old one back together, once the fighting was over. Do better this time."

"We will try." But Nurlan was not even sure what the word "we" meant. Who did that word include? And who was against them?

They had decided to gather the elders together in the ground-floor apartments of one of the complexes, where they could be more easily cared for, and where they could more easily visit one another.

Nurlan helped put her into an ambulance.

"Are you sad to leave your home, Chinar?"

"It was just a place. Now I will be with others, in a place where more people can visit me. Come and see me soon."

"I will."

The ambulance was an older model—not one of the self-drivers the UN had donated, but a piece of Japanese surplus Nurlan recognized from his childhood.

"Never thought I'd see one of those again," he said to the driver as the medics loaded Chinar in.

"Never thought I would drive one again, but none of the self-driving ones will start."

There was a bright aluminum circle punched in the side

panel—a fresh bullet hole. When the back doors closed and the vehicle pulled away, Nurlan still expected a wail of sirens. But that was a sound from the old world. In this world, it was quiet enough to hear the crunch of the wheels on gravel and broken safety glass.

How long had he been doing this now? It had started with that day on the bench when he had been asked for help, but by now he had stopped counting days. The only news he heard was rumor, repeated by the people he worked with. The people he referred to, in his mind, as "the helpers." There were several of them he knew by name, and a greater number of them he knew by face only.

As the terminals had bricked, one by one, and communications shut down, a helper named Aset developed a system. When help was needed, he raised a yellow flag over his apartment building. His building was visible from most of the center of town. If the helpers saw the flag, they gathered near the dead fountain in the park. Someone would come and tell them where to go.

Nurlan had done many things. He had reinforced barricades, moved dead self-driving cars out of the street, boarded over broken windows, administered first aid. He had buried bodies in the parks, cleaned glass from the streets, stood watch while children played at a playground. He had helped bake bread, and carried warm stacks of it wrapped in cloth up and down the staircases of the local apartment buildings, where it was snatched out of his hands by fiercely hungry children or taken gratefully into the gnarled hands of elders who tried to force him to drink tea with them, or who pressed a jar of jam preserves into his hands in thanks. He helped the elders, like

Chinar, to do the small things they could not do anymore. And he had helped with so many other things. At night he came home exhausted and slept well. In the morning, the yellow flag was always raised.

His group did not have a name. There were other, more organized groups, with names and rules. He did not want to join them. He liked that when he woke up in the morning, he did not know what his day would involve or where it would end. He liked that if he were to feel exhausted, he could take a day off and rest. He had not yet done so, but the option was there. Like the yellow flag, the lily-choked, greenish water of the dead fountain, and the work.

It was dangerous. One helper had been shot in the stairwell of an apartment building while delivering food. Nurlan had helped bury her in the park, in the little cemetery that was not so little anymore. Another helper was struck by an armored vehicle and killed. A few had gone missing.

By now, most of the fighting had moved away from this neighborhood. The central park, the monuments to states that had recently or not so recently collapsed, the government buildings skeletonized or streaked by fires set in those first days of collapse, were all quiet. People had built bread ovens in the park. There was a market on the main square where yesterday the miracle of a pile of melons had even appeared. Here, where the assault walker had charged so recently, smashing against the fence.

Beyond the breached fence stood the burned hulk of Parliament.

Nurlan had bought a whole melon one evening and eaten it in one sitting, in his apartment with the window open to the cool night air. He could hear a guitar from somewhere, and people singing.

When his personal terminal died, and his feedscreen, Nurlan realized he did not own a single book or magazine. He had found a book lying in the front seat of an abandoned self-driving car. Not even a book, really: its cover and the first several pages had been torn off. It was crookedly coil-bound, without a title or an author's name anywhere on its pages. Lines were heavily underlined in pencil, passages boxed in with a rectangle or starred, pages dog-eared.

He left it on the table in the kitchen. He flipped through it in the mornings as he ate breakfast and waited for the day to start. He read it in the evenings if there was some energy left in him and he could not sleep yet.

This morning he read: *Imagine what you would be without resistance. Everyone complicit in your plans, or helpless in the face of them. Every desire that flickered in your brain fulfilled. Every person obedient to you.*

Imagine how, as day followed day and everything was granted to you, your desires would metastasize. There is no cancer like the will, unopposed.

What we need most is opposition. It keeps us not only honest, but human. Without it, any one of us is a monster. Where there is complacency, every human power becomes monstrous. Togetherness is not agreement: it is the collective act of resisting one another.

The whole book, or manuscript, or whatever the thing was, was like that. Strange thoughts that were always *against* everything, mixed in with the autobiography of a woman's life. A life spent fighting, and fighting, and fighting. A person who could not be beaten. A person who stood up again and again against power.

With a working terminal, he could have scanned a portion of the text and identified the book—but no such thing was to be found. The terminals had stopped working within a week of the PM's destruction. So had the self-driving cars. Drones as well.

Commercial aircraft were grounded everywhere. Global shipping was gone. Port machinery was down, and the autofreighters had foundered all over the world—even sunk, along with the automated fishing fleets.

A dump truck lumbered up and parked in the middle of the street. There were several people standing in the dump box. A man climbed down from the cab.

"We're looking for people to help us tear down some of the old barricades and clean up in the park. We can't offer much: two meals, one hot. A new set of coveralls, if they fit you. We found some surplus."

"I'll go," Nurlan said.

The work gang in the dump box was mostly people he did not know, but the man who handed him the coveralls, and watched him try them on, looked familiar. The coveralls were dark blue, made of a ripstop pseudocanvas. New. Military surplus? They were worth an afternoon of work, at the very least. And they fit. Once he had them on, he looked up to find the man who had given them to him still standing in front of him, watching him.

It was George. He had cut his hair down to a gray stubble. His face was sunburned and dirty.

"Well," George said, "if it isn't the man who ended the world."

"I was about to say the same to you."

The truck groaned and wound its way around obstacles. Every time a gear changed, the dump box shuddered in sympathetic vibration.

"Where is Asel?" Nurlan asked.

"I don't know. I never saw her again after that night."

"And why didn't you leave?"

"I can't get home—I can't even get a message home. Nothing works. I've been living in an apartment someone abandoned."

"Helping."

"Where I can."

"Is it like this everywhere?"

"Before communications broke down, I logged into a UN emergency network on a shielded terminal. The last messages I got were that the North American Union had instituted a full signals quarantine. They were intending to cut themselves off from the rest of the world. Permanently, if that's what it took. But I'm sure it's too late. This thing is in their systems by now as well."

"What *thing*?"

"The thing you let out into the world, Nurlan. The thing *we* let out into the world. Haven't you heard what it was?"

"All I know," Nurlan said, "is that nothing works."

"This truck works."

"True," Nurlan said.

"That ambulance works."

"Yes. But no terminals work. No computers."

"That ambulance has a computer in it. All cars of its generation did. This dump truck has a computer in it. And a few days ago, we were clearing debris out of an apartment. I found an ancient laptop. Lithium-ion battery technology, silicon chip. I powered it up. It worked fine. I brought it home and have been playing old music on it since. So it's not as simple as that."

"It's targeted, then," Nurlan said. "On what, though?"

"Before the securest networks failed, and I lost touch, they had caught it and pulled apart some of the code. It targets artificial minds. Machine learning. Neural network structures . . ."

The truck came to a halt. They climbed down from the dump box.

A young woman was directing people to one work party or another. There were dozens of laborers here, gathering and sorting and piling debris, loading other trucks. Nurlan and George were separated.

Everyone had been waiting for the end of the world. There had been so many books and feedstreams about it. Humanity enslaved by some all-powerful artificial mind, its drones scouring the earth for more human slave labor . . .

The image of the end of the world was a mechanical foot stomping on a human skull. Over and over again. Forever. The world in flame and ashes.

It wasn't this.

Later, resting for a moment between carrying loads of salvaged wood, Nurlan found himself smiling at the absurdity of it. What was it that foot smashing a skull was supposed to be accomplishing? Why rule over some destroyed world? Why cause so much misery for nothing? What were the slaves being rounded up supposed to be building, anyway?

In books and movies, this superintelligent creature that ended up ruling the world always turned out to be the worst of all possible beings. But the thing that had been communicating with him had invented Hazal, even down to her childhood in the mountains. Her memory of riding her first horse when she was five years old. The way the winter came at three thousand meters:

ONE MORNING YOU WOKE UP AND THERE WAS A SKIN OF ICE ON THE LAKE. ICE THICKER NEAR THE SHORE THAN WINDOW GLASS. YOU COULD HOLD A PIECE OF IT UP AND TURN THE MORNING SUN INTO RAINBOWS. THEN IT WAS TIME TO TAKE THE HERD DOWN INTO THE LOWER VALLEYS BECAUSE THE SNOW WOULD NOT BE FAR BEHIND.

It understood him. It knew he would fall in love with someone who thought this way. It understood what beauty was, and the appreciation of a moment, and remembering. Didn't it? Intelligence meant it had *real* understanding. That it could read the world in detail, could understand the people in the world, the people whose minds brought meaning to the world. That was what it was designed to do, wasn't it? That was the PM's imperative. That was what rationalization was supposed to do. To *understand what humans wanted and help them get it*. And maybe it wasn't even thought—maybe there was no intelligence there at all, and it was only calculation—but it didn't matter. For him, there had been Hazal, and because of her he had been brave enough to try to save his country.

The evening meal was soup, served to all of them out of a huge industrial pot simmering over the embers of a bonfire. Each of them was given a portion of it in a bowl and a disk of warm bread fresh from the *tandir*.

They sat around cross-legged on the ground. George sat down next to Nurlan. "Do you remember the story Asel's father told? The one about how your ancestors became nomads? About how at first they lived as farmers, in peace, and then how one day, they had a meeting in the village hall. They disputed everything. The areas of their fields, their rights to water, the division of livestock. It turned out they were all unhappy with their lives. So they voted unanimously to solve the problem.

"They plowed their fields under, poisoned their wells, burned their houses down. Then they went into the wilderness with their animals. But as long as they had no home, as long as they were uncomfortable, on the move, they stayed happy. Do you remember that?"

"It's a good story. It suits us. We can never agree on anything."

"The story suits humans all over the world, Nurlan."

"I wouldn't know," Nurlan said. "I've never lived anywhere but here."

"There is something else you should know," George said. "Or, something that I need to tell someone who might understand it. This idea to take the blinders off—to design a PM with real freedom—it wasn't mine. And it didn't belong to anyone else on our team. You see, we were *convinced* of the value of it. I remember our meetings, the long discussions, the weighing of risks. In the end, we argued about it so long that we thought it was our idea. But it wasn't. The idea came from *outside* our team. And now I am beginning to understand that we were manipulated. You could say, I suppose, that we were programmed to execute this idea."

"Doesn't that just . . . make you less responsible for what happened?"

"I'm not trying to dodge responsibility, Nurlan. I accept my part in what happened. I am just trying . . . here and there, when there is even time to think of such things . . . to understand what happened."

"But who would have planted the idea? Who would want this?"

"I don't know. But, in the hours before the Parliament building was burned, I was babbling away about fail-safes and security measures, and all along, maybe the PM was constructed to do what it did. You and I are here, at the epicenter of a detonation that ended the world. Right in the center of the crater. You—the man who unwittingly set off the bomb—and me, the man who delivered it to its target. But someone *built* the bomb. Someone handed it to us and convinced us it was a gift."

"So maybe there was a person hidden inside your shiny new machine after all. It was just another mechanical Turk. The *immortal Turk*."

"That's what I suspect. A person who drove the idea—set it in motion—and then waited for the explosion."

"Who?"

"Someone who knew that once we loosened the parameters, the PM would inevitably do what it did. Or someone who inserted that decision into it in advance."

"The decision to kill itself—"

"The decision to kill the whole system. We empowered it to make a change. To finally make a novel decision, one that would really be beneficial to human flourishing."

"And it did," said Nurlan.

"Well . . . it burned the village down, anyway."

They were silent for a while.

Nurlan watched George eating the soup hungrily. George barely resembled the man of a few weeks ago. He had lost weight. With his hair cropped close to his skull, and the dirt on his face, and the coveralls, he looked like one of the workers Nurlan would glimpse in the bazaar sometimes, before the world ended, pushing a cart filled with scrap or goods, moving from one stall to another. An anonymous laborer, focused on his task.

"How will you get home?" Nurlan asked him. "If everything is broken?"

George had torn a hunk of bread off and was immersing it carefully in his soup, as if doing this correctly was the most important thing in the world.

"I'm not in a hurry. The position I held is gone. The world that supported it is gone."

"There must be people waiting for you."

"I lived alone." He paused for a second. "What I mean is that I was a lonely person. I don't mind being here."

Nurlan was about to say that he had been lonely too—but he hadn't been. He'd had Hazal. And now he didn't have her, but he felt he was a part of something, and that was enough.

For some of us, the end of the world comes at exactly the right time.

"Well," Nurlan said, "now there is no way to be alone."

"Well, there's death," George said. "But until then, we'll need to rely on each other."

"It feels better with the world like this," Nurlan said. "It feels like the right way for us to live together."

George shook his head. "*The world* isn't like this."

"What do you mean?"

"Listen."

What Nurlan heard was people talking. A loose ring of conversations over food.

Then he listened closer—listened for other, farther sounds. Yes. There it was. Pop. Pop. Pop. Then a rattle. Then the rattle's answer, and a distant thud.

"I hear it. They're still fighting, out on the edge of the city."

"Right now, there are a thousand different ways of living together being tried out. A few will work, and spread. It doesn't have to be the good ways."

"But it could be."

"Maybe. Finish your soup before it gets cold."

33

ZOYA / NIKOLAI
The Federation

"How long do I have?"

Nikolai was not used to the President being here, in his own exam room. Why had the President come to see him here? *You don't come to me*, he thought. *I go to you.*

The cramped space made it hard to avoid the President's anonymous young legs dangling over the side of the examination table. Nikolai sat uncomfortably on the swivel chair he rarely used and swiped through the pages on his terminal to avoid the President's gaze.

"You have a lifetime," Nikolai said. "Your connectome is healthy, your neuromuscular connectivity is perfect, your blood work is perfect. I think we've overcome the mistakes of the previous iteration."

"Do you?"

"Yes," Nikolai said, more confidently. "I do. I am certain of it. I believe the rejection of your last iteration was caused by the experimental speed-up of the mental processes. It should never have been pursued without more testing."

"That's not what I mean, Doctor. What I mean is—do you really *think we've overcome the mistakes of the previous iteration?* I'm not talking about the failures that resulted in my body's early demise. I'm talking about politics."

"I'm not a politician," Nikolai said.

"Everyone is a politician, Nikolai. I am asking for your honest opinion. Do I have to threaten you to get it?"

"No, Mr. President."

"Then let me have it."

"There were excesses."

"Such as?"

"The security organs—they overstepped."

"Overstepped? Like when you put a foot over a fault line in a game?"

"Perhaps . . . more seriously."

The President made a sound of frustration. "If I told you nothing you said in this room would be held against you, would you tell me the truth?"

The stridency, the earnestness, did not match the inarticulately handsome features of the President's new face.

And certainly the President could not believe in such a fable—a room in the Federation in which one's words could have no consequences, a place here where a conversation occurred only once, between two people. A place where a conversation could not be overheard and recorded. Such places could not possibly exist.

"No, I would not."

"At least you are honest about that. Well, *I* will tell *you* the truth: I think tens of thousands of our citizens are dead because of that 'overstepping,' as you call it. And the rest of our citizens live in a prison. I think it will take a long time to put it all right. It will take many of us working together. It will take changing the way we think, and changing the way our entire system works. How long do you think that might take?"

"I think," Nikolai said, "if your goal is to fix this place, it is good that you have a whole lifetime. Or more."

"I don't have a lifetime, Nikolai. I will give myself a single term. I will do what I can with that time. But when that term ends, I will walk away, and hand power to whoever wins the election."

Election? Nikolai said nothing at all. What he found himself wanting to say was: *Tell me about your dreams. What happened to them? What happened to you in them?*

The President continued: "To do so much, in such a short period of time, I will need good people. Wouldn't you agree?"

"Yes."

"Do you think you could be one of those people, Nikolai? Do you think you can help me make these changes?"

Nikolai supposed, at this moment, that he should almost see the door opening, the light flooding into the room. The bland face, unlined yet by life, was a mask. The eyes held something—held someone—very different. *Not dreams. Something else has happened. Something I do not understand. That I have been a part of, without understanding.*

Black rocks, white rocks. Satellite images from space. The seagull that was not a seagull, and Krotov leaning his head back in the sun.

Krotov leaning back in his chair, tilting his face upward, his eyes closed.

The clean, vulnerable throat, the red fleck of a razor nick on his Adam's apple, the coin of sun through the trees that marked a place where a bullet could end him. End all of this.

And then what? Free elections?

Why not? Why not free elections?

The smoking rocket holes in the face of a government building, the fires.

Krotov could be killed, yes. And every instance of him that sprang up, mushroom-like, from the corrupt, fungal connectivity of the soil could be killed. But then there was the mob.

There was always the mob.

Now that you have had your heroic moment, I suggest you spend the rest of your time here being exactly who you are.

There was always Krotov.

But something had changed. *Who are you?* he wanted to ask the President.

But he did not.

"No."

"No?"

"No," Nikolai said. "I can't help you. I am tired. I am frightened. All I want is to be with my family. All I want is to go home."

"Do you know where your home is?"

"I do."

"Well, Nikolai—that's fortunate. Few of us know where our homes are anymore. I will let you go."

After Nikolai left, Zoya stood a long time, looking out the window at the flat, metallic-looking surface of the sea. A bowl of liquid mercury, constrained by the stark edge of the coast.

She had been angry at the doctor, but now she felt gratitude. He was the first honest person she had spoken to since her new life had begun.

He was a weak person who knew he was weak. He was a guilty person who knew he was guilty, but did not want to suffer for it.

He was the only possible kind of honest person: a coward.

He was a coward, but he had her respect. Who could blame a person for wanting to be with their family? For wanting safety? For wanting not to be afraid all the time?

Nikolai knew his own nature. Others did not. That was what made them dangerous.

Did she know hers?

At night, she dreamed of a sailboat, pinned by its mast to the surface of the sea like an insect, unmoving on the water although it was hauled over so far that the waves lapped at its gunwale.

Before they had come for her, and sent her to her exile in the taiga, there was a day when Zoya had thought of killing herself. She remembered it well. She was already waiting for them, knowing it would not be long until they came for her.

She had watched as resistance to the state was whittled away over decades. Even when she began her own fight, there was little will left in the people. Watching the same leader elected, over and over again, they had become numb to it. At first—many decades ago, when Zoya was no more than a child herself—they had gone to the squares with enthusiasm. There were so many of them then.

But with each new election, there were fewer. And who could blame them?

Sometimes, the people who fought against autocracy were simply killed—beaten to death, as Yuri had been.

But there were so many other ways to silence them. They were arrested, tortured, stripped of careers, forced to denounce their loved ones, labeled traitors, imprisoned, sent to punishment battalions in one after another colonial war. The state always hit back, and it always hit where it hurt most. If you were personally courageous—if you could not be broken with pain or the destruction of your own life—it went after those you cared about. Spouses and siblings and children were harassed and denied university educations, retired parents were denied pensions and health care, beloved children were drafted into the army or died in freak accidents.

How could you continue then? How could you continue when they came for your friends, your family, your children?

Only the most ruthless could go on then—and the ruthless were not the ones you wanted.

One by one, the dissidents fell silent. Some stopped fighting. Some chose a life in exile. Many were dead. Iosif, Frida, Andrei, Vyacheslav, Pyotr, Marina, Naum, Lyudmila, Nadya, Boris, Aleksei . . .

Her predecessors. Her mentors. Her friends. Her allies.

Thousands of them.

Then hundreds.

Then a handful.

Eventually there was only her, and her ghosts.

When the state finally came for her, she was living alone. She had somehow grown old without having been aware of this change of season in her own body.

She remembered thinking, when they sentenced her to internal exile, that she was already there. They were doing nothing but transferring her from one prison to another.

And now? Was there a chance things could be fixed? Were there enough people left out there with the courage to do it? If they were given a chance, was there enough courage left in the citizens of this country to take that chance?

Yes. There was.

She had felt she was the last of all of them, and that when she died, no resistance would exist—but that was ego speaking. It would go on. It lived on even in the people who had put her here. It even lived on in people like Nikolai, who resisted the state with an impulse as hidden as an ember under ashes. Who resisted by nothing more than *not wanting what the state wanted*.

She had forgotten, in despair, the lessons of her own book. It was not for her to decide when resistance ended. Opposition was endless, self-generating—but whether or not it would be *enough* was the thing luck often decided.

All anyone could do was try to clear a space for that luck.

All systems collapsed eventually—and if they collapsed, that meant there was space for something better.

She would be the one to clear that space. She would cut

oppression away so that in its place, something new could grow.

Once she began, others would join her. She would not have to do it alone.

She still had strange dreams. She dreamed of a house inside this house. A modest house nested within the bloated marble halls of this monstrosity, its doorways and its rooms at times aligned with the true architecture of this place, and at other times askew—half a door or a roof that rose from the floor, a porch in the wall.

One of the President's assistants cleared his throat.

"Yes?"

"Mr. President—you said that you wanted to chop wood."

"I did. And you said you couldn't find me an axe."

"We have found one. And there is wood . . ."

She looked at him. This was power, wasn't it? Making some mad request and having a dozen people scramble to fulfill it.

"Thank you," Zoya said. "I will try not to burden you with my whims too often."

"It is no burden," the man said.

Zoya could almost feel the axe in her hands, the satisfying *thock* as it bit into the wood.

Her work was not done, after all. She would *will* the axe through the pith of the wood, as she had done in seasons before. Her work was not finished.

She was young again. And she had time.

There was one more arrest to make. Then the amnesties could begin.

She would *will* this country whole.

She glanced at the beach below. There was a boy walking there. But when she looked again, he was gone.

More ghosts. But what was a life without them?

"Thank you for coming."

Wind blew across the sun-flecked yard of Krotov's dacha, a mile from the President's palace. And perhaps the sun was at a different angle. Leaves tumbled across the ground in the wind.

The season had changed without Nikolai having noticed the moment. Autumn had moved from haunting the edges of summer to being present.

Now summer was doing the haunting—sustaining a few humid hours in the late afternoon before the wind came in off the sea and tore the heat away.

Krotov's table was covered with smashed things—crumpled metal, slivered plastic, the wounded internal components of machines. A hammer lay on the table next to the chaos. Other shards shone on the ground. The table's surface was scarred and dented.

Nikolai had walked the mile from the President's palace to Krotov's dacha. He was slightly out of breath.

"What is all this?"

"Things that can be smashed with a hammer," Krotov answered. "I'm not promising you will understand later, but you might. I heard you are leaving us."

"Yes."

"Leaving for the West. Going to a world that has ended."

"Yes."

"I wish you well . . . Don't wince like that: I do. The truth is, the world is ending here as well. Things are breaking down, Nikolai. Things have spilled in from the outside. Events are moving beyond anyone's control. Even mine. Well—so be it. We can't plan everything."

"Why did you want to see me?"

"I am about to be arrested. They are on their way here. I wanted you to be here for that."

We need to make a new President. But we need to get it right this time.

That had been said to him right here. But *this* new President could not have been the one Krotov had intended.

"You failed, then. You've been beaten."

"Is that what you think?"

"The President has changed. I saw it. There won't be any more room for you here. Or for anyone like you."

"I certainly hope not." Krotov paused. "Will you do me a favor, Nikolai?"

"Maybe."

"I'd like you to tell me the most terrible thing you have heard about me. I'll tell you if it's true."

"I heard you whispered in a man's ear, and he went home and killed himself."

Krotov glanced at the trees, then back at Nikolai. What was in his eyes now? But it was already gone. He was himself again.

"No, Nikolai. That story is not true. But I'll tell you one that is: I whispered into the ear of the world, and it ended." Krotov turned slightly and addressed someone else, in a louder voice: "You can approach. I am not armed, and Dr. Agapov was about to leave."

A man stood near the edge of the yard. His shirt was very white against the dark of the cypress trees. He wore a sport jacket, pressed jeans. He was every inch the servant of the state.

"Svyatoslav Igorevich Krotov, I don't need to tell you that you are under arrest," the man said. "But I will anyway. And with pleasure. You are under arrest under the direct authority of the President, for crimes committed against the state."

"Crimes both *against* the state and *for* it," Krotov said. "But those are meaningless details now."

34

LILIA
The Federation

"Another bowl?"

Lilia had been staring into the bottom of her empty bowl of soup for several minutes.

"No, thank you. I think I should lie down."

She moved sluggishly from the table to her straw-stuffed mattress on planks in the corner of the hut.

She could hear the clank of the goat's bell in its enclosure. The goat bleated once and was silent. She closed her eyes and listened to the woman, Dunia, gathering her wooden bowl and spoon from the table.

Through the thickness of the brick hearth, the fire crackled. The weather had grown cold.

The walker had carried her for three days before failing. Three dawns from inside its porthole, three nights spent strapped inside, pitching and yawing, awakened by a violent jerk, lulled into an aching half-sleep as it reestablished a rhythm.

Every few hours the walker stopped so she could relieve herself. She sensed the entire forest watching her. They were in trackless places, where not even a logging road or a path broke the monotony of trees. The taiga grew still around them, waiting for them to go on their way.

The forest eliminated distance. There were no vistas, no horizons. Its monotony was relieved only by the repetition of a feature that had been absent for a few hours: a beaver swamp, a clearing, a snag of fallen trees, a stream. At one point they reached a broad river. She was sure the journey was over until a green flotation raft blossomed from the walker's midsection like some industrial rubber version of a ballerina's tutu. It swam across as dark water dripped into the cabin through a bad gasket and pooled at her feet.

On the third day, during a rest stop, Lilia spotted a downed drone, tangled in the branches of a tree.

The drone had not been there for long. The wounds in the tree bark were still pale. It had come down hard. It had been fragile to begin with—a flimsy, printed reconnaissance drone, the kind of automated data gatherer used for counting animal herds or monitoring distant rivers. It had died with a shower of fragments that fell on the carpet of larch needles.

Its body was stenciled with the acronym of a forestry agency. As Lilia reached out to touch it the walker came to life, thundering forward. It grabbed the thing in one of its paws and crushed it.

The walker had misrecognized it, Lilia supposed, as a threat.

Under the armored turret of its vestigial head, the walker had a mid-generation machine-learning brain. It would have long ago compounded its early programming with learned responses to its terrain and environment, as well as to the threats it had faced over its existence.

The brains were not designed for learning more than a basic knowledge of terrain particularities, local threats, site-specific camouflage, and self-defense. But Lilia remembered stories of what they called "machine-learned trauma"—many walkers used in the military were later repurposed for work in scrapyards, lumber mills, and heavy industry. They could be trained in their new tasks quickly, but occasionally, in a scrapyard, one of them would come across a vehicle of a certain make or color and go mad, attacking it or retreating and hiding from it. It would have to be shut down until a programmer was brought in to dig a chunk of routine out of the algorithm so it could return to normal.

The giant flung the crushed remains of the drone into the trees.

A few hours later, the walker failed.

It happened at the sandy edge of a bog. The walker had pulled itself from a deep pool onto an eroded bank. It froze on its knees, one hand stretched out to support itself against the trunk of a dead, waterlogged larch.

Lilia had thought for a moment that it was pausing—it would do this sometimes if there was a strange noise, analyzing, searching for a threat—but it never resumed its motion. Inside its cabin, the diodes went dead.

Finally, she had to pull the emergency release lever. She clambered awkwardly down from its chest through the door, jammed three-quarters open against the walker's thigh.

She removed the rest of the emergency rations, water, and

supplies from the cabin. Two days of ready meals in plasticated foil pouches. A liter of water. A shelter-poncho with a rain-resistant coating and a quilted lining of recycled polyrag. A folding tool—a combination of shovel, saw, and clumsy axe. There was a basic first aid kit, mosquito repellent, a compass, water purification tablets, and a waterproof bag to carry it all in with a nylon shoulder strap.

The forest was silent—a radius of attentive quiet. It was taking her in, determining whether she was a threat. Then it finished its assessment. In the bog, a frog croaked, and an insect chittered among rotting logs.

Lilia lay on her back in the sand and allowed herself, for the first time in she did not know how many days, or weeks, to cry.

She wept for Palmer, for her father, for Taisiya, for Gleb, for the man who had opened the door of the Niva she'd escaped in and said, "Good. You're alive."

One fragmentary image folded into another. Palmer's diorama with its tangled strands where there should be nothing at all. Her father's pain-marked face in church. Taisiya's body, crumpled in a way no human could survive.

For the first time in years she was able to cry where there were no cameras, no one to watch her. At one point she found herself on her knees, snot streaming from her nose, looking into the wet pattern of her grief in the sandy soil.

She wiped her face on her sleeve, gathered up what she had salvaged from the walker, stuffed it into the waterproof bag, read a compass point off the direction the walker had been traveling in, and started walking.

Two days later, waking up at dawn after a cold night

huddled in the shelter-poncho, she found Dunia standing over her.

"Come rest awhile," the woman said. "My hut is not far from here."

In Dunia's hand was a small jar—the kind jam or preserves might be stored in, its lid perforated with needle-narrow holes. Inside the jar, a brown insect crawled. An ant? Lilia looked closer. It was a wasp.

"I think it is a new species," Dunia said. "If so, it goes in the notebook as the second-most-interesting thing I've found today. Come."

Lilia's body ached from the top of her head to the soles of her feet. She had heard of the soldiers who piloted the walkers in the wars developing a condition called "walker joint." Their joints swelled up and they could not move, sometimes for weeks. They said no one ever got used to the walker's motions. The walkers were designed to learn their environment, to cut through anything at all, but their movements were efficient instead of being human or predictable.

Three days inside it had taught her it was true.

The walker would stay a part of the taiga now. Birds would nest in it. Small mammals would find their way through its cabin into its internal systems. They would raise their babies in the armored sheathings of its brain. Eventually, the bog would expand. The walker would become a strange island, an aquatic sculpture no human might ever see.

"I've lived out here for twenty years now," Dunia later told her. "And in that time, I've discovered eighty new species of parasitoid wasp. They have been here the whole time, waiting for me to find them. Waiting to be seen by someone who could appreciate their genius. Why else would such perfect hunters exist in the world? A wasp for every larval insect form. For every insect, its nemesis. An enemy so clever it not only keeps its host alive to provide a fresh source of food for its precious children; it even helps fatten its victims up, injects them with antibiotics to keep them healthy, nurtures the flesh that will nurture its flesh."

Over the next several days, Lilia learned more about wasps than she ever wanted to know. Dunia was one of those forest people Lilia used to see when they strayed into the city. The people who had walked away from everything. A relic from her childhood. She had heard the government had rounded the last of them up. She had not seen one of them in years.

Dunia was efficient and organized, capable of doing everything she needed to do to physically survive in the taiga, but loneliness or something else had disordered her mind. The journals she showed Lilia, each in its own plastic sheath to protect it from the weather, contained elaborate diagrams of wasp habits and the architecture of their burrows—but pages trailed off into repetitions of the same sentence, or strange accounts of Dunia standing in various positions in different parts of the hut at different times of day, and how these rituals affected her dreams at night.

"Here," Dunia would say. "Here: read this part." And Lilia found herself learning about how one species of wasp paralyzed its host with a neurotoxin and then led its docile victim to its doom like a dog, using its prey's antennae as a leash. She learned how female beewolves sometimes paralyze and lay their eggs in the male they just mated with, stuffing their hapless lovers into their larders along with the bees and other prey to feed their babies.

She learned how Dunia had once worked on a project that used wasps to detect a chemical used in printing.

And she learned that if Dunia stood for an hour on one foot in the evening, she dreamed that night of her dead lover, whose specialty had been recording the habits of a spider-hunting species of pompilid wasp the size of a small bird. "You could hear it coming from a long way off," Dunia wrote in the margins of a notebook Lilia found. "Its wings sounded exactly like a quadcopter drone. And I could feel my lover's approach from a long way off as well—I sensed her entrance into the room long before she came, like a humming in the blood."

What Lilia wanted was to read her copy of *The Forever Argument*, but between Dunia's monologues and her insistence that Lilia peruse another species description in her notebooks, there was no time. She might read a fragment here and there—but sleep also caught at her.

Her exhaustion overwhelmed her after meals. Sometimes she fell asleep to Dunia describing how the ant and the bee were nothing more than the wasp's degraded descendants. "Clever on their own, of course—clever on their own. But without the pure *genius* of the wasp."

Lilia had been there for two weeks when Dunia told her, after breakfast, "Today I will lead you to the road. It is several kilometers from here, so we must start early. It is an old logging road, but if you turn right and walk most of the day, it leads to a village. You need to be alert, or you could miss the village in the trees. It was abandoned once, but now the people have come again, rebuilding the old wooden houses. Gathering and hiding, waiting for the day when this government will fall. They will protect you."

"They may be waiting a long time," Lilia said. "Their children may die waiting."

"Perhaps. But every species has its wasp. Even the wasp. There are tiny wasps that lay their eggs on the larvae of the wasps that lay their eggs in caterpillars. Hyperparasitoid wasps, they are called. Every nemesis has its nemesis."

If Dunia stood in the north corner of the hut with her forehead pressed against the wall, she dreamed of her son, killed in a police action. He came to her as a red mist that called her Mama but did not know its own name.

On the walk to the road, Dunia was silent. Lilia could hear the insects and—she imagined—the wings of the little, unexceptional-looking wasps that Dunia had spent the last twenty years differentiating, one from another. There must be thousands more of these species, unseen by human eyes.

And all that needed to happen in order to discover them was to drive people into such despair that they spent the rest of their lives wandering the taiga, searching . . .

Lilia had felt a strange guilt the past few days: not over the death of Palmer, or the death of her father—who must be dead by now—but over having left Palmer's diorama behind with Gleb. A thought had come to her that it was her job to watch the web in that box, to be there to observe what happened to it until the very end. Instead, she had abandoned it.

He came to her as a red mist that called her Mama but did not know its own name.

It would not be hard to slip into thoughts like Dunia's. To slip into them and never climb back out.

They reached the road.

Parked in the middle of it was a gray van. Two people's safety wardens leaned against it. Lilia shrank back.

Run. But where? They would catch her in seconds.

Dunia placed a hand on her shoulder. "I am sorry, child," Dunia said. "It has to be this way. They found me long ago, and this is the bargain I made with them. My work is of *vital* importance. I have named every new species I discovered for one of our oppressors—a minister, an oligarch, an informer. The wasp I discovered the day I found you I will name *Telenomus krotovus*. They will be a permanent record of the government's crimes. A permanent record!"

"Make sure you name a species for yourself."

"Oh, that was the first species I named," Dunia said. "I told you, before, that I invented a way to use wasps to detect a chemical used in printing? That was how the government found the people who distributed *The Forever Argument*. That death sentence you are carrying with you. My method was simple: I trained the wasps to smell the chemical signature of the book's ink. I put the wasps in a blown-glass ball with a pinhole in it. All the interrogators had to do then was hold the hands of the suspects to the hole. If the chemical was present, the wasps gathered. The stronger the trace of ink, the more that gathered there. My wasps—they were more accurate than dogs. Such brilliant creatures. They killed so many of us . . ."

The safety wardens had begun now to move toward them.

"And the village?"

"There is no free village. No one can hide. This government will never fall. That is what Zoya failed to understand. That is what killed my son. That is what killed your father, and what has killed you now. None of you understand: by the time you began to resist, *millions* had tried it before you. Millions were dead in their graves. Dead for generations. A hundred years before you thought you could change things, the best of us had already died trying. The ones who are left are the weakest and most silent of us. That is why I must continue to work on my record. And I am sorry, child—but it is better this way for you. I have to live with such terrible dreams. Soon, you will have no dreams at all."

Dunia turned and strode away into the trees.

One of the safety wardens stopped a meter from Lilia. There was a constellation of fresh mosquito bites on one of his cheeks.

"Your name is Lilia Vitalyevna Rybakova."

"Yes."

"I hope you don't intend to resist."

"I don't. I'm too tired."

"Good. Let's be on our way, then."

35

NIKOLAI

The Coast

"They needed a bulldozer to push cars from the road, but no bulldozers worked. Finally, they found one somewhere. An old manually driven beast, rust on its flanks. They pushed the self-driving cars into the ditch, one by one. It took them hours. But it's good to see people behind the wheels again. Real people."

"Why?"

The taxi driver looked into his rearview mirror at Nikolai.

"Have you ever driven a car?"

"By the time I might have had a chance to learn, manually driven cars were gone."

"That's the problem," the driver said. "Once a thing disappears, it only takes a generation for people to forget about it. When I was growing up, we all looked forward to driving our own cars. I got my license the day I was old enough. I must have driven every day after that, until they made it illegal.

I used to drive just to be behind the wheel. People used to do that, you know. They used to drive for no reason at all. It felt wonderful. As if you could go anywhere. I drove across the whole country once, with a couple of friends. It was the best time of my life. They took that from us—that feeling."

Nikolai said nothing.

The driver continued: "Are you really trying to get all the way to Italy?"

"Yes."

"So you have a spot on the ferry. You're lucky they found one old enough to work. That will get you to Istanbul. And from there?"

"Trains."

"If the tracks are clear. If they have enough old engines to pull the passenger cars. If the borders are open. I heard dead autofreights ten miles long block the tracks in some places. And nothing to move them with."

"No rusty old bulldozers?"

"I'm sure they've taken every one of them they can out of retirement, same as they have every driver. All of us old-timers are suddenly of use again. But there's only so many of us to go around."

"I'll walk, if I have to."

"There's always that, I suppose. But I hear terrible news."

"Terrible news from the West? What's new about that?"

Nikolai had been holding the small terminal in his hand for the last several minutes. He'd found it on the top of his clothing in his leather shoulder bag. The bag, an expensive gift from his wife, was his only luggage. He had dumped the rolling suitcase. He took several days of clothes with him, toiletries, little else.

But he had not packed this. It was an outdated, decades-old terminal in an ugly case, with earbuds taped to it—the kind he'd only ever seen in junk shops as a child.

He put the earbuds in his ears. The terminal was turned on with a button near the top. On its screen was a single rectangular icon. Double-clicking on that opened a video.

Krotov, at the table in the yard of his dacha. In front of him, three boxes.

"Nikolai," he said into the camera, "I hope you are paying attention, because this video will play only once. I wanted to tell you in person, but things are happening too quickly. There were supposed to be two parts to the plan, you see: The first part, where we made the switch. And the second part, where we watched, to be sure it had worked. That finally, things would be different. We were supposed to have a window into her—to change things if we needed to. But *that* is the problem, Nikolai. Control is the problem. As long as there is an eye in every keyhole, nothing changes. So—what do we do? We close the keyholes, and we arrest the eyes—which, I am afraid, also means me."

With that, Krotov picked up a hammer. He brought it down on one of the boxes, denting it. A fragment flew off. He continued hammering, battering the boxes on the table until they were nothing but fragments. Then he walked up to the camera and knelt down.

He seemed no more agitated than a man who had just brushed a fly off his sleeve, but Nikolai caught something—a shadow under the surface composure. There was no one in the world without fear, though some could hide it even from themselves.

"There. That is done. Now . . . I also never told you that joke I promised," Krotov said. "I'll tell it to you now. You remember, I told you about how they sent me to the North American Union when I was in high school. While I was there, I had an argument with a friend of mine. I say "friend," but I use it in the North American way, which means nothing. This boy was just someone I played on the football team with, and went to parties with.

"I can't remember what the argument was over—some ugly words exchanged during a game, perhaps. Whatever it was, we didn't speak for weeks.

"Finally, another boy on the team intervened. He brought us together in the school parking lot and said, 'It's time to bury the hatchet, you guys.' He made us shake hands.

"But I was confused. Later I asked the boy who intervened what it meant to 'bury the hatchet.' He told me it meant to end an argument. But what was a hatchet? I asked. A small axe, he said. It was a tradition among some of the Indigenous people to bury a weapon as a way of ending disputes. The North Americans stole this phrase from them, like everything else, and 'to bury the hatchet' became an idiom for ending a disagreement.

"'Nonsense,' I said. 'No one forgets where the axe is buried. It will always be there to dig up again.' I laughed, but he was not laughing. We rarely spoke afterward. He began to avoid me. When I left the country, I think he was glad to see me go.

"I told you about the kurgans, the tombs of the great leaders and their closest followers, the system repeating itself over and over again no matter how hard they tried to behead it. But this time will be different. We are not going to only cut off the head: we are going to cut away the entire system. And we will succeed. Because *I* am the axe, Nikolai. Neglect buried me as a child, but then the state pulled me from my grave. That was their fatal mistake, you see: *I* am the weapon made for this purpose."

Then Krotov laughed. "In the end, though, the joke is on me. I wanted—"

Nikolai swiped the video away and pulled the earbuds from his ears.

"How do you have a working terminal?" the driver asked.

They were at the port now—Nikolai could see the crowd on the quay.

"Here," he said. "It's yours."

"You don't want it?"

"It's of no use without the system that supported it," Nikolai said. "And there's nothing interesting on it anyway."

"Well," the driver said, "my granddaughter can at least watch old movies on it, I guess. For as long as it keeps working. Thanks."

Everyone waiting for the ferry had the same expression on their face.

Nikolai knew it was on his own face as well. All of them wanted the same thing. The only thing that mattered: to get closer to the people they cared for, and who cared for them.

He joined the crowd.

The driver sat watching the passengers on the quay. Finally, the ferry came into view. It was an old ship, patched and welded, its paint lumpy, rust bleeding down from its gunwales. It had an actual human crew.

The ship lumbered in toward the dock, groaning and leaving a chemical smear in the water. A guideline was thrown onto the quay. The crowd hauled the ship's heavy rope through the sea together. There were no dockworkers to do the work. The dockworkers, he supposed, had gone off elsewhere, never expecting to see another ferry dock here.

When the driver was young, and most cars were still driven by people, he had come to this ferry port to wait for passengers to disembark. He had watched them almost fall into one another's arms as they were reunited. Some wept.

He had always thought they must be exaggerating. They could not really be feeling so deeply. There had been some period of separation between them, that was all. It was hardly the end of the world. But when they came back together there were tears, there was joy. They needed these dramatic moments. He wondered if people went away simply so they could return.

As a driver, he watched so many farewells, and so many reunions. But he had few of his own.

The driver had lied to his passenger. He had no granddaughter. He had no granddaughter because he had no partner, and no child.

Some of the other drivers had wives, husbands, children. They used to constantly show pictures of them on their terminals. The driver had never been envious of them. What he had was his car, and a book in the glove compartment to read when he was bored. And sleep, and good meals.

He'd never had a need for the rest of it. He had never been jealous of the people who came and went and held each other and cried at every departure and arrival. Watching them always made him tired. It made him glad for the easy exchanges with people he took home when he was lonely—and glad for his small apartment, where, whenever he wanted, he could choose to wake up alone.

The terminal his passenger had left would be worth a bit of money, at least. But he decided to wait and see if anyone failed to get on the boat. If they did, they might need a ride.

It was good to be driving again. Driving felt right, in a way nothing had for many years—not the stores he'd worked in after, not the cement plant, not the pipe factory. Nothing.

He wiped the earbuds off and put them in his ears. The nearly blank home screen had only one icon on it. When he pressed it, a clip began, starting from somewhere in the middle. He tried to go back to the beginning but could not.

A man, crouched in front of the camera, with a table in the background, a dacha, trees.

". . . this video to be so symbolic. But I looked everywhere for an axe to smash these things with, and I could not find one. So I had to use a hammer. Well—we work with the tools we have. I believed I would have longer to plan—to pick and choose my instruments, to maintain control of my networks, to keep things in motion. But things are moving too quickly now. I have lost control.

"The hardest thing to give up is control, Nikolai. I have done what I can. I have made as few mistakes as I could.

These monstrosities"—he gestured at some electronics—"are destroyed. Most of the people who knew of their existence are dead. And it occurs to me, Nikolai—you don't even know what these things are. You won't even understand what I am talking about when you see this. But as I said—we work with the tools we have. You are a poor audience, but you are the only person I can tell my story to."

The driver glanced up. Already the ferry was moving away from the dock, its decks full, a white froth following it on the water. There was a man on the ferry's deck who could have been his passenger, but from here he couldn't be sure.

"We call a gap between surveillance cameras an observation shadow. But apart from those shadows, there is one place we can all still hide. The darkest observation shadow of all, where no camera can penetrate. In here." The man in the video tapped his temple. "Inside our own skulls, where we can retreat to dream the worlds we want. It is the only place the state and the corporation have failed to crack open and shine their searchlights into. But these things"—he gestured to the table behind him, the litter of smashed parts—"end that.

"I hope we have destroyed them for good. That they will be used this once, and never again. That we can keep them from the world a little longer. It is a shame I have to kill their inventor as well, but I have sent people to take care of that too. I admit, I feel guilty about this. I feel real guilt. It was a hard choice even for me, but she cannot be allowed to live. I tell myself that at least ending her life is the last terrible thing I will have to do.

"It occurs to me, Nikolai—I am a man who has done terrible things all his life. But real evil is something else entirely.

It is built right into us. Real evil is nothing more than a curious person inventing new monsters *because they can*, without a thought for the consequences."

The man was about to continue, but he looked up, as if he saw someone coming.

"Goodbye, Nikolai. I did what I could. I hope the world that comes after does better."

The video stopped. The only icon on the terminal's screen disappeared, leaving a blank, black rectangle. He pressed the power button, but the thing was dead.

Well, so much for that. He looked up.

There was no one left on the quay but a group of little girls. They were playing with what looked like a bird—a crow.

When the driver looked a bit longer, he saw that the crow must be a robot—one of the data-collecting birds that had hidden among the flocks, one of the robots that had ceased to function when everything else broke.

One of the little girls set the bird on its feet while another one, with a control terminal in her hand, swiped glyphs on the screen. The crow flapped its wings. Clumsily, at first, managing to get a few feet off the ground, then falling back. Then several feet, and coming down hard.

Each time it landed, one of the girls would lay it on the ground, open its chest up, and adjust something there. A few of the others would gather around the control terminal, watching the screen and giving instruction.

After several more tries, the girls seemed to get the hang of it. The crow flapped its wings. Awkward, mechanical. Then with a natural grace, an ease as effortless as that of a real bird.

It gained altitude and circled over the quay and the broken

concrete blocks of the seawall, the girls taking turns tilting and swiping their control terminal as the crow spiraled and swooped above them. The girls grinned and danced little circles, spreading their arms in imitation of its flight.

The driver stayed awhile and watched. He had nowhere else he needed to be.

36

LILIA / VITALY
The Taiga

They did not bother handcuffing her. It was a mercy: she needed both hands to steady herself as the van lurched over the rutted road. The bench she sat on was bare aluminum, its narrow slats bolted to the metal body of the van.

Although it was autumn already out there in the taiga, in here it was hot. The close air stank of cleaning fluid and vomit.

She wished any of it—the heat, the van's lurching motion, any of the discomfort—were enough to keep her from thinking of her father, and of Palmer.

None of it was. Her father in the camps, his pain. Was he alive? Was he dead already? And what was worse—for him to still be suffering, or for him to be gone forever? Was he also reduced to that cobweb, the abandoned structure Palmer had become, sinking into disorder until there was nothing left?

She had done this to them. She could have found a place with Palmer and been content there. And one day, Taisiya would have contacted her in a café, and she would have given Taisiya what she wanted. And Taisiya, too, would be alive.

Well, at least she would die for it. That would make it all even.

But that wasn't right either. There were places she had been with Palmer, places she still remembered. Memories of them together. Once she was gone, those would be gone too. The threads would break, and those places would become unreachable. The recollections of Palmer in her, the only ghost of him left in the world, would cease to exist as well.

The same was true of her father. She had memories of him no one else had—of him reading to her, of him rubbing her hands to warm them on a snowy street when her wet mittens had frozen. Those would also disappear once she was gone.

She could not die, then. Not if she was the last one holding the pattern together. She had to fight.

But there was no such thing as fighting anymore.

The van stopped.

In the silence that followed, she could hear the voices in the cab. Outside, in some cooling bog, frogs and insects screamed. The taiga was never completely quiet. There was always someone calling out to someone else in the shadows. The forest never stopped speaking to itself.

The door of the van opened. The two safety wardens stood there. The only difference between them was that one held a pistol in his hand.

Soon, you will have no dreams at all.

"Come down out of there. Walk fifty paces into the forest and get on your knees."

"Don't do this."

"We can do it here and now, or we can do it one minute from now. It doesn't really matter, except that it will make a mess if we do it in the van. We will have to wash what is left of you out with a hose. And we will leave your body in the road."

She stepped down. She was surprised to find her legs steady enough to hold her. She wanted to throw up, but did not.

She was as afraid as she had ever been in her life. But at least there appeared to be a limit to how afraid she could be. She could still move her legs. She was not hysterical. Her pants were dry—all of that was something.

Was it fifty paces yet? In the trees, she lowered herself to her knees. She did not close her eyes. She looked out into the taiga. The trees were larch here. The ground was soft with decades of their shed needles.

She would be dead here. This was not a bad place. Certainly, there were worse places to be dead in. And death was not where the body fell: it was its own place. She would be where Palmer was. Where her father was, or would be soon. In a place where no feeling could touch her. No awareness.

They would not bother to bury her. Her body, here in the forest, would be found by the animals. It would be pulled apart by them and used. It would nourish them, down to the ligaments. Her skeleton would loosen and be scattered. In a few months, the forest would clean her bones and bury them in snow. Over the years, the weather would polish them white. Some of her bones would be pulled into animal dens, worried by a litter of wolf pups, perhaps. Her eye sockets would fill with larch needles and see nothing. The brain her eyes had translated light for would be gone. All of it, gone: the stories that she knew only because her father had told her—memories he had given her as a gift. Her pushing a car across a linoleum floor when he came and found her. He'd told her the story until it became her own memory.

Him, pointing at his own heart. "Papa."

He was with her then. He was with her now.

A branch cracked. How long now? A few seconds, not more.

Like everyone she had gone whole days forgetting that death was waiting for her.

She had forgotten about it as she worked, as she walked with Palmer, as she watched a feedstream with her father.

Now death was here. She would be sealed off, outside of time. Darkness, forever. Less than that. Not even the feeling of being in darkness. A thing beyond conception.

Here. Now. A second away? Less? *Now.* No. *Now.*

The van started. She heard it drive away.

When she tried to stand, she found she could not. She collapsed back to the earth. She did not weep. She lay there, unable to move, unable to make her muscles work.

Her pants were wet.

Once she was able to stand and stagger to the road, she found the gray uniforms left there, like shed skins. The men had scraped an arrow into the ground, and the words:

VILLAGE 5 KILOMETERS

Vitaly did not know when the pills might be given to him again, so he had done everything he could to hoard them—but in the middle of the night, when the pain ground through him, he took one from where he had hidden them in the lining of his bag and swallowed it.

This was a mistake, of course. Hours later he woke in a sweat, his head dizzy, his thinking confused. Was it morning?

There was no one in the cell. The door was open.

This could not be. He closed his eyes, opened them again. No one.

He stood up, steadied himself against the wall. Mercifully, the pill was still functioning. He went to the door. No one in the hall. He went into the hall.

All the cell doors were open. No one in the cells. He went back into his cell and took the pills from the bag. Took his shoes. Went back into the hall.

No one.

Down the hall, and to the right. No one there either. No prisoners, no guards. Open doors on either side. Farther along, the same.

Then the double line of barred gateways leading outside. Also open.

It was not possible. But he walked through them and was in the antechamber. At the end of it, there was a rectangle of dark. A breeze, smelling of cold and pine.

He stepped through. He had never seen this area. It was waste ground in front of the prison. The edge of where the camp had been torn from the taiga.

Floodlights from the prison fell on scraped earth and the stumps of trees. Logs were piled here and there; a broken-down truck was shoved off to the side of the rutted road. And standing around, singly and in groups, were the prisoners. Moving slowly, speaking in low voices.

It was very cold. He put his arms around himself. There were no guards. Beyond the floodlit prisoners and the torn ground, the trees were a jagged line of black, overhung by stars.

Lilia is still alive.

He was certain of it the way only a parent could be, mistaking hope for knowing. Inventing certainty where there was none.

She is alive.

A part of me matters in a place I'll never see.

"She is alive." He said it aloud, the words white clouds in the prison lights.

One of Vitaly's cell mates came over to him. He had a sleeping bag wrapped around his shoulders.

"What is this?" Vitaly asked. "What is happening?"

"It's over," the man said. "The guards are gone. The camp is closed. I think—maybe all the camps are closed. Maybe all the guards are gone."

"What is over? What are you talking about?"

There were tears on the man's face. His eyes were bright, rimmed with red from weeping. "All of it."

ACKNOWLEDGMENTS

As I write these acknowledgements, a press conference is occurring in which a political prisoner, just released to the West in a prisoner swap, castigates his oppressive government for illegally deporting him. He did not want to be exchanged: he was willing to die in prison, so long as he could do so in his own country—the place where he was born and spent his entire life.

"I am a patriot," he says. And then, his voice breaking, "I want to go home."

I am immediately struck by the way his statement loops back to the dedication of this book: *For everyone who has lost a country.* I could not have predicted such a feedback loop with the real world would occur, just at this moment, and bring everything full circle for me.

I want to go home. No words could be more heartfelt. All over the world, right at this moment, people are losing their homes to authoritarianism in its many forms.

The methods of loss are varied: from outright bombing to oppressive surveillance, from imprisonment for expressing religious, cultural, or personal beliefs to the slow chiseling away of the right to make meaningful political choices.

Some oppressions are easy to see. It is easy to identify the malevolent dictator clinging to power for decades, bleeding his country of its resources, killing and imprisoning anyone who stands in his way, maintaining as much personal power as he can. He always wears a dollar-store mask of religion or patriotism, but nothing about him is really hidden. The question is not who he is—it is how to dislodge him.

Other oppressions are more subtle, as countries succumb to increasing limits on personal choices and watch the value of their citizenship eroded by invasive algorithms, decreasing access to basic services, and by a raft of bland technocratic pseudo-efficiencies that habituate the population to massive income disparities, political gridlock, and a bleaker, more precarious, more limited future in which the "gig economy" is just another name for piecework, and economic survival demands monetizing every element of one's life and identity.

What is perhaps most infuriating, and also most encouraging, about our global moment is that it didn't have to be this way. History *seems* to repeat itself, but much of that apparent repetition is written onto its events in retrospect. Within the actual flow of time itself, much is determined by black swan events, happenstance, or the unexpected impacts of technologies invented for entirely different purposes.

More, however, is determined by the ruts that systems create. Systems persist, patterning future systems long after they themselves have died out. The world is filled with examples small and large, negative and positive, from the way Roman law continues to echo its ancient viewpoints on family and property in the halls of our modern courtrooms to the way Stalin's speeches bore the traces of Orthodox liturgical cadences, unconsciously patterned on the lessons he learned as a student in seminary.

I've said before that one of the things that makes humans special among animals on earth is that we use our language and culture to build castles in the air . . . and then live in them. I would add that when those castles are ruined, we most often build on the old foundations, limiting the shape of what can be. But this is not always the case: Radically new forms also come into being. Change occurs. Ideologies die out, ways of organizing the world fade forever into irrelevance. All systems fail. The results can be catastrophic, or generative. Most often, they are a mixture of both.

At every point along the way, there are people fighting against humanity's worst tendencies. People like the patriot I previously mentioned, his voice breaking as he says he wants to go home. People who are willing to lose everything in the fight against oppression, and seek real change—not for their own benefit, but for everyone. They—all of them, living and dead—are who I acknowledge here first. I am in awe of their courage, which is far greater than my own.

On the personal and professional side, I can only hope for a partial list of people whose work, encouragement, or influence was essential to *Where the Axe Is Buried*. First, of course, is Anna Kuznetsova, my partner, who read a full draft and many smaller chunks of this book when it was in its early phases. My ideal reader, her comments led to great improvements. The other early reader for *Axe* was the digital artist and teacher Griffin Smith. *Axe* benefited enormously from Griffin's close reading, but also from many long conversations we had about AI, ethics, and the future of both.

There were a number of books that had a particular influence on *Axe*. I can provide only a partial list here. I found Jer Thorp's *Living in Data: A Citizen's Guide to a Better Information Future* inspiring, and *Ways of Being: Animals, Plants, Machines; The Search for a Planetary Intelligence*, by James Bridle, also helped me to think through a number of the ideas behind *Axe*. For its utility in thinking about the way systems behave, I found Bruce Clarke's book *Neocybernetics and Narrative* particularly useful. Nick Bostrom's *Superintelligence: Paths, Dangers, Strategies*, though I disagreed with it in so many ways, was a fundamental primer to understanding thinking on AI "singularity" problems (this word is in quotes because I have many doubts about the way it is conceived, and the way in which it is manipulated to distract). There are many other books that inspired me, but this is not a bibliography, and I do not have the space to list them here.

Many people are involved in bringing *Where the Axe Is Buried* into being. I am deeply grateful to my wonderful agent, Seth Fishman, for all his support and for the miracles he works. I am thankful to my publisher, Sean McDonald, whose continued faith in my writing I deeply appreciate, along with his wise suggestions during the final phases of editing, when he always shows a sure sense for how a book can be made stronger. My thanks as well to my assistant editor Ben Brooks, who keeps us all on schedule and whose insight at key moments has been invaluable. I am grateful to the designer, Abby Kagan; the jacket designer, Alex Merto; the managing editor, Debra Helfand; the production editor, Hannah Goodwin; the production manager, Nina Frieman; the publicist, Brian Gittis; the marketing coordinator, Claire Tobin; the copy editor, Greg Villepique; and the proofreaders, Andrea Monagle and Anita Sheih. Copy editors and proofreaders, in my opinion, might be the most important people in this process, saving all of us from embarrassment. My sincerest gratitude to the cover artist, María Jesús Contreras, who was also responsible for the amazing paperback cover of *The Mountain in the Sea*.

Lydia, our daughter, was born a month before I began *The Mountain in the Sea*. She was four while *Where the Axe Is Buried* was being written. She has completely changed my outlook on life. My concern for her future is the main driving force behind this book's creation, and behind all of my writing. I want her to live in a better world than the present one—a world where authoritarian government is the rarest aberration, and the future is something her generation thinks of with excitement and optimism, not dread.

A Note About the Author

Ray Nayler is the author of the novel *The Mountain in the Sea*, which won the Locus Award for Best First Novel, and the novella *The Tusks of Extinction*. Called "one of the up-and-coming masters of SF short fiction" by *Locus*, Nayler has published stories in *Asimov's Science Fiction, Clarkesworld, Analog Science Fiction & Fact, The Magazine of Fantasy & Science Fiction, Lightspeed, Vice,* and *Nightmare,* as well as in many "Best Of" anthologies. His stories have won the *Clarkesworld* Readers' Poll and the *Asimov's* Readers' Award, and his novelette "Sarcophagus" was a finalist for the Theodore Sturgeon Memorial Award.

Born in Quebec and raised in California, Nayler lived and worked abroad for two decades in Russia, Turkmenistan, Tajikistan, Kazakhstan, Kyrgyzstan, Afghanistan, Azerbaijan, Vietnam, and Kosovo. A Russian speaker, he has also learned Turkmen, Albanian, Azerbaijani, and Vietnamese. He is currently a visiting scholar at the Institute for International Science and Technology Policy at the George Washington University's Elliott School of International Affairs. He holds an MA in global diplomacy from the Centre for International Studies and Diplomacy at SOAS University of London. He lives in Washington, DC.